Modern
Athletic Training

Ken Rawlinson

The Athletic Institute
200 Castlewood Street
North Palm Beach, FL 33408
U.S.A.

Library of Congress Catalog Card Number 80-69602
ISBN 0-876-70-061-X

II

ACKNOWLEDGEMENTS

CONSULTATION AND REVIEW OF MANUSCRIPT

Dr. Don Robinson, M.D.
Team Physician
Oklahoma, University'

Dr. Don H. O'Donoghue, M.D.
Team Orthopedic Surgeon
Oklahoma, University

CONTRIBUTORS TO THIS EDITION

Scott Anderson, A.T., C.
Assistant Head Athletic Trainer
Oklahoma, University

Bill Chambers, A.T., C.
President, National Athletic Trainers Association
Head Athletic Trainer
Fullerton Junior College
Fullerton, California

Joe Gieck, E.D.D., A.T., C.
Head Athletic Trainer
University of Virginia at Charlottesville

Larry Hall, A.T., C.
Athletic Trainer
Sabino High School
Tucson, Arizona

Ted Layne, R.P.T., A.T., C.
Head Athletic Trainer
Colorado University

Charles Martin, A.T., C.
Head Athletic Trainer
Northeast Louisiana

Terry Middleswarth, A.T., C.
Head Athletic Trainer
University of North Carolina at Wilmington

Don Moseley, A.T., C.
Athletic Trainer
San Angelo, Texas

Dan Quinn, A.T., C.
Athletic Trainer
Norman High Shool
Norman, Oklahoma

LaVada Ingle
Supervisor, Jefferson Cafeteria
Oklahoma University

JoAnne Crane, R.D.
Goddard Health Center
Oklahoma, University

Warren Harper
Assistant Football Coach
Oklahoma, University

PHOTOGRAPHY BY:

Ken Neptune
Athletic Filming Coordinator
Oklahoma, University

MANUSCRIPT TYPED BY:

Sharon Beery

We came from diverse backgrounds and a common interest: a love of sports. After four years, we left with an appreciation of sports and love of a man who taught more than sports. Honesty, integrity, dedication, and loyalty were but a few of the qualities which he so fondly taught us.

He served his profession with these same attributes. Those of us who were privileged to have been under his caring wing became better professionals, but above all, better human beings as a result of it.

Scott Anderson
Bill Chambers
Joe Geick
Larry Hall
Ted Layne
Charles Martin
Terry Middleswarth
Don Moseley
Dan Pickett
Dan Quinn

Let us not forget those people who had the same love and devotion to Ken who chose not to find a career in athletic training. Ken felt that many of his students would have made fine trainers, but let them find their own future. We are all part of the same family.

A WORD FROM THE PUBLISHER

Interest in athletic trauma is higher today than at any time in the history of American sport. As a consequence, the profession of the sports trainer has come under close scrutiny and evaluation.

As these staff positions open up due to retirement or expansion of the nation's school system, our secondary schools and colleges are demanding better trained, better qualified, personnel to fill these important positions. And with this growing demand there is a persistent need to seek knowledge from the experienced trainer to supplement the formal academic education.

For many years, there was little literature on the subject of athletic training. At the same time, as the athletic programs in our schools and colleges grew in size and complexity, the athletic coach too often was asked to assume responsibilities far beyond his limited training in the area of injury recognition, treatment and - above all - prevention.

Two decades ago the late Ken Rawlinson, athletic trainer at the University of Oklahoma, wrote a book which, with the passage of the years, has come to be recognized as a classic of its kind. Rawlinson was a dedicated student of sports trauma and an astute veteran of the athletic training room. In his monumental work he answered clearly and lucidly virtually every question that can be asked by the young trainer or coach concerning athletic conditioning, prevention of injury, recognition of the severity of an athletic trauma, its treatment, and the rehabilitation of the athlete, both mentally and physically.

During a long and distinguished career, Mr. Rawlinson accumulated the experience and knowledge to make *Modern Athletic Training* the definitive work on the proper care of the athlete. His techniques, tested and proved in the crucible of top-drawer collegiate competition, gained him the same measure of national prominence that his Oklahoma University teams earned on the athletic fields and courts.

In this, a new and completely revised edition of *Modern Athletic Training*, the knowledge and experience which Mr. Rawlinson shared with his associates has been richly enhanced out of the knowledge and experience gained by one of his disciples, Mr. Dan Pickett, present head athletic trainer for the University of Oklahoma Athletic Department. Mr. Pickett and a team of colleagues in the training profession have updated the original Rawlinson manuscript to include new and improved techniques and therapies.

For its part in making this new and revised edition of a classic text available to a new generation of readers, The Athletic Institute is most grateful to the National Football League Charities for its co-sponsorship of *Modern Athletic Training*.

Howard J. Bruns
President & Chief Executive Officer
The Athletic Institute

Don Bushore
Executive Director
The Athletic Institute

NATA CODE OF ETHICS

National Athletic Trainers Association
June 1980

PREAMBLE - PURPOSE - N.A.T.A. OBJECTIVE

One outstanding characteristic of a profession is that its members are dedicated to rendering service to humanity. Also, they are committed to the improvement of standards of performance. In becoming a member of the athletic training profession, the individual assumes obligations and responsibilities to conduct himself in accordance with its ideals and standards. These are set forth in the Constitution and By-laws and are emphasized in the CODE OF ETHICS. Any athletic trainer who does not feel that he/she can or does not deem it necessary to comply with the principles set forth in the CODE should have no place in this profession.

The members of the athletic training profession must adhere to the highest standards of conduct in carrying out their significant role in athletic programs at all levels. It is for this reason that the Board of Directors of the National Athletic Trainers Association has continually revised the CODE which has been in effect since June, 1957. *

In approving the Code, the Board of Directors recognizes and believes that, unless the standards and principles that are set forth in this document are accepted in good faith and followed sincerely, it will not be effective in continuing to improve the contributions of the profession and its members to athletics and sports medicine.

Ethics is generally considered as conduct in keeping with moral duty and making the right actions relative to ideal principles. Let it be understood that all members of the National Athletic Trainers Association will understand and apply the principles set forth in this CODE and make every effort to do the right thing at the right time to the best of their ability and judgement.

PURPOSE

The purpose of this CODE is to clarify the ethical and approved professional practices as distinguished from those that might prove harmful or detrimental and to instill into the members of the association the value and importance of the athletic trainer's role.

OBJECTIVES

The stated objectives of the National Athletic Trainers Association in its constitution are:

1. To advance, encourage, and improve the athletic training profession in all its phases and to promote a better working relationship among those persons interested in the problems of training.

2. To develop further the ability of each of its members.

3. To better serve the common interest of its members by providing a means for free exchange of ideas within the profession.

4. To enable the members to become better acquainted personally through casual good fellowship.

ARTICLE I - BASIC PRINCIPLES

The essential basic principles of this CODE are Honesty, Integrity and Loyalty. Athletic trainers who reflect these characteristics will be a credit to the association, to the institution they represent and to themselves.

When a person becomes a member of this association he/she assumes certain obligations and responsibilities. A trainer whose conduct is not in accordance with the principles set forth in the following sections shall be considered in violation of the CODE.

Section 1 - Athletics in General

An athletic trainer shall show no discrimination in his/her efforts while performing his/her duties.

Section 2 - Drugs

The membership of the National Athletic Trainers Association does not condone the unauthorized and/or non-therapeutic use of drugs. The association recognizes that the best and safest program is comprised of good conditioning and athletic training principles.

Section 3 - Testimonials and Endorsements

In any endorsement in which the trainer's name and/or reference to the athletic training profession is included, the wording and illustration, including any implications of the endorsement, shall be such that no discredit to the training profession may be construed. (Any endorsement that is not in keeping with the highest principles and standards of the athletic training profession shall be considered unethical). The N.A.T.A. name, logo, trademark and/or insignia may not be used in any testimonials and/or endorsement - service, products, programs, publications and facilities - by individual members or groups of members of the association.

Section 4 - Sportsmanship

Members of this association shall not condone, engage in or defend unsportsmanlike practices.

Section 5 - Fellow Trainers

Any trainer who, by his/her conduct or comments, publicly discredits or lowers the dignity of members of his profession is guilty of breach of ethics.

Section 6 - Membership

It is unethical for a member to sponsor for membership in the National Athletic Trainers Association a candidate whom he does not know and with whose qualifications he/she is not familiar.

Section 7 - Solicitation of Patients for Fee

It is unethical for a member who is actively engaged in the profession and/or teaching in an approved Education Curriculum to solicit personally or to use any form of advertising for the purpose of soliciting, for fees, "outside" patients for a clinic or athletic training facility.

ARTICLE II - EDUCATIONAL PREPARATION AND CERTIFICATION

Any certified member of this association must be considered an educator if he/she is involved with the professional preparation of students pursuing National Athletic Trainers Association Certification through any of the approved certification routes.

Section 1 - Educational Standards

The athletic trainer-educator must adhere to the educational standards and criteria set forth by this Association.

Section 2 - Selection of Students

The athletic trainer-educator who is responsible for the selection of students for admission into a professional preparation program must insure that policies are non-discriminatory with respect to race, color, sex, or national origin.

Section 3 - Publication and Representation

Publication and representation of the professional preparation program by the athletic trainer-educator must accurately reflect the program offered.

Section 4 - Evaluation of Students

Evaluation of student achievement by the athletic trainer-educator must be done in a prudent manner.

Section 5 - Recommendation for Certification

It is unethical for a member to knowingly recommend a candidate for the national certification examination who has not fulfilled all eligibility requirements as specified by the Board of Certification.

Section 6 - Confidentiality of National Certification Examinations

It is unethical for any member to reproduce in written form, or reveal in any other manner, any part of the written or oral-practical examination for the purpose of aiding certification candidates in passing the examination.

ARTICLE III - ENFORCEMENT

Section 1 - Reporting of Unethical Conduct

Any member of the association who becomes aware of conduct that he/she considers unethical and that he/she believes warrants investigation, shall report the incident(s) in writing to the President and the Executive Director of the association, who will in turn initiate investigations through the Ethics Committee. He/she shall include in the communication all pertinent data.

Section 2 - Investigation and Action

In accordance with the by-laws of the association, the Ethics Committee investigates reported incidents of unethical conduct and if, in the judgement of a majority of the committee members it finds that the accused person has violated the National Athletic Trainers Association Code of Ethics, it communicates its decision to the accused and to the Board of Directors in writing and recommends to the Board one of the following disciplinary actions:

1. **Letter of Censure**
Copies to immediate supervisor and district director.

2. **Period of Probation:** (This shall be determined by the board of directors.)
During the period of probation the member shall not be eligible for any of the following:
   a. Hold an office at any level in the association.
   b. Represent N.A.T.A. in the capacity of liaison with another organization.

3. **Initiate Procedure for Cancellation of Membership**

Section 3 - Action by the Board of Directors

This decision of the Board of Directors in Code of Ethics is final, except that if the decision is to initiate cancellation of membership, this shall be done as prescribed in Article VI, Sections 1 and 2 of the Constitution.

*1971, 1973, 1974, 1976, 1977, 1978, 1979, 1980.

NATIONAL ATHLETIC TRAINERS ASSOCIATION

RESUME

Authorization:
The National Athletic Trainers Association was formed in June 1950 at Kansas City, Missouri.

Purpose:
The stated objectives of the Association are to educate, advance, encourage and improve the Athletic Training Profession in all of its phases and to promote a better working relationship among those interested in and concerned with the problems of Athletic Training.

Officers:

President
William H. Chambers
Athletic Department
Fullerton Jr. College
Fullerton, CA 92634

Executive Director
Otho Davis
Philadelphia Eagles
Veterans Stadium
Philadelphia, PA 19148

Board of Directors:
Jack Baynes, Northeastern University
Richard Malacrea, Princeton University
Andy Clawson, The Citadel
Bob Behnke, Indiana State University
Frank Randall, Iowa State University
Cash Birdwell, Southern Methodist University
Dale Mildenberger, Utah State University
Don Chu, California State University at Hayward
Bobby Barton, Eastern Kentucky University
Gary Craner, Boise State University

Activities:
The Board of Directors conducts business meetings semi-annually; committee meetings are scheduled as required.

The Association has an approved certification examination. This examination, developed with the cooperation of the Professional Examination Service of the American Public Health Association, is administered by the N.A.T.A. Board of Certification. The examination is offered on a regional basis.

The Professional Education Committee has approved the curriculum programs at schools offering a program of study in Athletic Training. The schools currently offering an N.A.T.A. approved curriculum in Athletic Training are as follows:

Approved N.A.T.A. Curriculums
(1) Bachelor's degree level curriculum
(2) Master's degree level curriculum
(3) High School faculty instructional program

Arizona:
UNIVERSITY OF ARIZONA (2)
Department of Physical Education
Tucson, AZ 85721 (Dr. Gary Delforge)

ARIZONA STATE UNIVERSITY (1)
Department of Health, Physical Education and Recreation
Tempe, AZ 85281 (Joanne Dunnock)

California:
CALIFORNIA STATE UNIVERSITY, FULLERTON (1)
Department of Health, Physical Education and Recreation
Fullerton, CA 92634 (Jerry Lloyd)

CALIFORNIA STATE UNIVERSITY, LONG BEACH (1)
Department of Physical Education
Long Beach, CA 98040 (Dan Bailey)

CALIFORNIA STATE UNIVERSITY, NORTHRIDGE (1)
Department of Physical Education and Athletics
Northridge, CA 91324 (Larry P. Krock)

CALIFORNIA STATE UNIVERSITY, SACRAMENTO (1)
Men's Intercollegiate Athletics
Sacramento, CA 95819 (Doris Fennessy)

Delaware:
UNIVERSITY OF DELAWARE (1)
Department of Physical Education and Athletics
Newark, DE 19711 (Dr. C. Roy Rylander)

Illinois:
EASTERN ILLINOIS UNIVERSITY (2)
School of Health, Physical Education and Recreation
Charleston, IL 61920 (Dennis Aten)

NORTHWESTERN UNIVERSITY (3)
School of Medicine
Center for Sports Medicine
303 E. Chicago Avenue
Evanston, IL 60611 (Richard Hoover)

UNIVERSITY OF ILLINOIS - URBANA (1)
College of Applied Life Studies
Department of Physical Education
Urbana, IL 61801 (Dr. Rollin Wright)

WESTERN ILLINOIS UNIVERSITY (1)
College of Health, Physical Education and Recreation
Macomb, IL 61455 (Valerie J. Lindbloom)

Indiana:
BALL STATE UNIVERSITY (1)
Department of Men's Physical Education
Muncie, IN 47306 (James C. Dickerson)

INDIANA UNIVERSITY (1,2)
School of Health, Physical Education and Recreation
Bloomington, IN 47401 (John Schrader)

INDIANA STATE UNIVERSITY (1,2)
School of Health, Physical Education and Recreation
Terre Haute, IN 47809
(Dr. Robert Behnke - Graduate)
(Dr. Kenneth Knight - Undergraduate)

PURDUE UNIVERSITY (1)
Department of Physical Education, Health, and Recreation Studies
Mackey Arena
West Lafayette, IN 47907 (Dennis Miller)

Iowa:
UNIVERSITY OF IOWA (1)
Department of Physical Education for Men: Field House
Iowa City, IA 52242 (Dr. Louis E. Alley, Chairman/Danny T. Foster)

Kentucky:
EASTERN KENTUCKY UNIVERSITY (1)
School of Health, Physical Education, Recreation and Athletics
Richmond, KY 40475 (Dr. Robert M. Barton and Ms. Darcy D. Shiver)

Louisiana:
LOUISIANA STATE UNIVERSITY (1)
123 Huey P. Long Fieldhouse
Department of Health, Physical Education and Recreation
Baton Rouge, LA 70803 (Dr. Marty Broussard)

Massachusetts:
NORTHEASTERN UNIVERSITY (1)
Department of Physical Education
Boston-Bouve College
Boston, MA 02115 (Kerkor Kassabian or Dr. Carl S. Christensen, Chairman)

SPRINGFIELD COLLEGE (1)
Division of Health, Physical Education and Recreation
Springfield, MA 01109 (Sherrod W. Shaw)

Michigan:
CENTRAL MICHIGAN UNIVERSITY (1)
Physical Education Department
Mount Pleasant, MI 48859 (Linda Treadway)

GRAND VALLEY STATE COLLEGE (1)
Department of Physical Education and Recreation
Allendale, MI 49401 (Dr. George MacDonald)

WESTERN MICHIGAN UNIVERSITY (2)
Department of Health, Physical Education and Recreation
Kalamazoo, MI 49009 (Jack Jones)

Minnesota:
MANKATO STATE UNIVERSITY (1)
Physical Education Department
Mankato, MN 56001 (Gordon Graham)

Mississippi:
UNIVERSITY OF SOUTHERN MISSISSIPPI (1)
Department of Athletic Administration and Coaching
Hattiesburg, MS 39401 (James B. Gallaspy)

Missouri:
SOUTHWEST MISSOURI STATE UNIVERSITY (1)
Hammons Center
901 S. National
Springfield, MO 65802 (Ivan Milton or Gary Ward)

NATA ASSOCIATION

Montana:
UNIVERSITY OF MONTANA (1)
Department of Health, Physical Education and Recreation
Missoula, MT 59801 (Dr. Walter C. Schwank or Naseby Rhinehart)

Nebraska:
UNIVERSITY OF NEBRASKA-LINCOLN (1)
University Health Center
Lincoln, NE 68588 (Ronald E. LaRue)

New Mexico:
UNIVERSITY OF NEW MEXICO (1)
Department of Health, Physical Education and Recreation
Albuquerque, NM 87131 (L.F. Diehm)

New York:
STATE UNIVERSITY COLLEGE AT BROCKPORT (1)
Undergraduate Physical Education Unit
Brockport, NY 14420 (Dorothy Cohen)

STATE UNIVERSITY COLLEGE AT CORTLAND (1)
Division of Health, Physical Education and Recreation
Cortland, NY 13045 (John Sciera/Tom Syracuse)

ITHACA COLLEGE (1)
Department of Health, Physical Education and Recreation
Ithaca, NY 14850 (Ken Scriber)

North Carolina:
APPALACHIAN STATE UNIVERSITY (1)
Department of Health, Physical Education and Recreation
Boone, NC 28608 (Ron Kanoy)

EAST CAROLINA UNIVERSITY (1)
Department of Health, Physical Education, Recreation and Safety Sports Medicine
Program
Greenville, NC 27834 (Rod Compton, Dr. Rick Barnes or Dr. Ray Martinez)

STATE OF NORTH CAROLINA (3)
Department of Public Instruction
Division of Sports Medicine
Raleigh, NC 27602 (Dr. Al Proctor)

UNIVERSITY OF NORTH CAROLINA (2)
Department of Physical Education
Chapel Hill, NC 27514 (Dan Hooker)

North Dakota:
NORTH DAKOTA STATE UNIVERSITY (1)
Department of Physical Education and Athletics
Fargo, ND 58102 (Dr. Denis Isrow)

UNIVERSITY OF NORTH DAKOTA (1)
Department of Health, Physical Education and Recreation
Grand Forks, ND 58201 (A.G. Edwards)

Ohio:
BOWLING GREEN STATE UNIVERSITY (1)
Department of Health and Physical Education
Memorial Hall
Bowling Green, OH 43403 (Robert Livengood)

OHIO UNIVERSITY (1)
School of Health, Physical Education and Recreation
Athens, OH 45701 (Charles Vosler)

TOLEDO UNIVERSITY (1)
Department of Physical Education
Toledo, OH 43606 (James D. Nice)

Oregon:
OREGON STATE UNIVERSITY (1)
Physical Education Department
Corvallis, OR 97331 (Richard F. Irvin)

PORTLAND STATE UNIVERSITY (1,2)
Department of Physical Education
Portland, OR 97207 (Leo Marty)

Pennsylvania:
EAST STROUDSBURG STATE COLLEGE (1)
Koehler Fieldhouse
East Stroudsburg, PA 18301 (Lois E. Wagner or John R. Thatcher)

LOCK HAVEN STATE COLLEGE (1)
School of Health, Physical Education and Recreation
Lock Haven, PA 17745 (David J. Tomasi)

THE PENNSYLVANIA STATE UNIVERSITY (1)
College of Health, Physical Education and Recreation
131 White Building
University Park, PA 16802 (John Powell)

NATA ASSOCIATION

UNIVERSITY OF PITTSBURGH (1)
Health, Physical Education and Recreation
Pittsburgh, PA 16057 (Charles Weinmann)

SLIPPERY ROCK STATE COLLEGE (1)
Health Sciences Department
Slippery Rock, PA 16057 (Dr. James R. Pennell)

WEST CHESTER STATE COLLEGE (1)
Physical Education Department
School of Health and Physical Education
West Chester, PA 19380 (Phillip Donley)

South Dakota:
SOUTH DAKOTA STATE UNIVERSITY (1)
Department of Health, Physical Education and Recreation
Brookings, SD 57107 (Dr. Jim Booher)

Texas:
LAMAR UNIVERSITY (1)
Department of Intercollegiate Athletics
P.O. Box 10066, Lamar Station
Beaumont, TX 77710 (Paul Zeek)

SOUTHWEST TEXAS STATE UNIVERSITY (1)
Department of Health and Physical Education
San Marcos, TX 78666 (Dr. Bobby Patton)

STEPHEN F. AUSTIN STATE UNIVERSITY (1)
Department of Health and Physical Education
Nacogdoches, TX 79562

TEXAS CHRISTIAN UNIVERSITY (1)
Department of Athletics
Fort Worth, TX 76129 (Ross Bailey)

Utah:
BRIGHAM YOUNG UNIVERSITY (1)
Department of Physical Education
Provo, UT 84602 (Marvin Roberson/Dr. Earlene Durrant)

Vermont:
UNIVERSITY OF VERMONT (1)
Intercollegiate Athletics and Physical Education Department
Patrick Gymnasium
Burlington, VT 05401 (Roger Bryant)

Virginia:
UNIVERSITY OF VIRGINIA (2)
Athletic Department
Charlottesville, VA 22903 (Dr. Joe H. Gieck)

Washington:
WASHINGTON STATE UNIVERSITY (1)
Department of Physical Education for Men
Pullman, WA 99163 (Dr. Douglas Sebold)

West Virginia:
WEST VIRGINIA UNIVERSITY (1)
Department of Professional Physical Education
Morgantown, WV 26505 (John Spiker)

NATA ASSOCIATION

Publication:
   "**Athletic Training**" *The Journal of the National Athletic Trainers' Association* is published quarterly, namely - Spring, Summer, Fall and Winter.

National Meeting:
   The N.A.T.A. Annual Meeting and Clinical Symposium is scheduled for the second week of June each year.

Representation:
   The Association is represented at the following meetings each year:

American Academy of Pediatrics

American Alliance for Health, Physical Education, Recreation and
   Dance

American College Health Association

American College of Sports Medicine

American Corrective Therapy Association

American Physical Therapy Association

American Society for Testing and Materials

Joint Commission on Competitive Safeguards and Medical Aspects of
   Sports

National Association for Girls and Women in Sports

National Association of Collegiate Directors of Athletics

National Association of Intercollegiate Athletics

National Collegiate Athletic Association Football Rules Committee

National Federation of State High School Associations

National Head and Neck Injury Registry

National Operating Committee on Standards for Athletic Equipment

Sports Safety and Health Care Society

Committee Chairmen

Audio - Visual Aids
Robert Burkardt
Wabash College
Crawfordsville, IN 47933

International Games
Lewis Crowl
5207 J Street
Sacramento, CA 95827

Career Information and Services
Charles Demers
Deerfield Academy
Deerfield, MA 01342

Journal
Kenneth Wolfert
Miami University
Oxford, OH 45056

Certification
Rod Moore
Valparaiso University
Valparaiso, IN 46383

Memorial Resolutions
James Rudd, Football Office
Kansas State University
Manhattan, KS 66502

Drug Education
John Wells
Mars Hill College
Mars Hill, NC 28754

National Convention
Fred Hoover, Athletic Departr
Clemson University
Clemson, SC 29131

Ethics
L.F. "Tow" Diehm
University of New Mexico
Albuquerque, NM 87131

Placement
Craig Sink
North Carolina State University
Raleigh, NC 27607

Grants and Scholarships
William E. Newell
Purdue University
West Lafayette, IN 47907

Licensure
Bob Behnke
Indiana State University
Terre Haute, IN 47809

History and Archives
Michael O'Shea
Miami University
Coral Gables, FL 33124

Professional Education
John Schrader
Indiana University
Bloomington, IN 47901

Honor Awards
George Sullivan
University of Nebraska
Lincoln, NE 68508

Research and Injury
John Powell
Pennsylvania State University
University Park, PA 16802

My main purpose in writing this book is to gather together the information, know-how, and techniques from my own experience and from what I have learned from so many gracious trainers and doctors in the past. I am deeply cognizant of and grateful all their help and only hope that this book may be of value to present and future trainers.

Ken Rawlinson

PREFACE

It was my privilege to have known, worked with, and enjoyed a close personal relationship with Ken Rawlinson from the day of his arrival at Oklahoma University in February 1953 until his death 26 years later. I watched the development of the first edition of *Modern Athletic Training* in 1961 from concept to publication and came to appreciate the meticulous care and total dedication that went into the work. He checked and cross-checked with respect to the traditional methods, but always with a mind open to accept newer techniques as they proved out effective.

Ken's burning ambition was to produce a classic of its kind, and succeeded. He wrote a book so rich in detail that the athletic trainer could very well turn to it as a daily reference guide. It contained an exhaustive compilation of treatment details for every conceivable condition. He believed devoutly that the physician was his bulwark of support and never presumed upon medical decisions. Armed with a wealth of personal experience, he could distinguish readily between those trauma that needed the service of a physician and those which did not, and he never hesitated to seek advice in borderline situations.

So we find ourselves approaching a new edition of Ken Rawlinson's book revised and updated by Oklahoma University Head Trainer Dan Pickett, who trained under the keen eye and infinite patience of Mr. Rawlinson. Dan's concepts are very similar to Ken's. In the twenty years since the original edition came off the press there have been some modifications and improvement in training techniques, and Dan Pickett has incorporated them in this new edition. What is remarkable, however, is how well the original text has worn. Indeed, in so many respects, Ken Rawlinson was ahead of his time.

Modern Athletic Training is an excellent guide to the management of the athlete's health. It leans heavily on prevention, addresses itself to the daily living habits of the athletes, and insists upon early recognition and treatment of injuries.

The athletic trainer and coach will find here a wealth of material, all designed to improve upon the care of the athlete. *This is the bottom line.*

Don H. O'Donoghue, M.D.
217 Pasteur Medical Building
1111 North Lee
Oklahoma City, Oklahoma 73103

LIST OF FIGURES

TABLE OF CONTENTS

I

The Trainer In Modern Athletics

The background of athletic training is long and illustrious. It had its start with the ancient Greek and Roman athletic contests, as evidenced in our archeological museums. Artists of the time found inspiration in scenes on the gymnasium, palestra, track and field. Vases, our most important record, reflect the various phases of the life of the athlete. Bronze and marble sculptures, gems, and coins also add to our knowledge. Recorded on these vases are many instances of the aryballos (oil flask), strigil (instrument for removing oil and dust from the body after exercise), and sponges. Other specific scenes shown on vases include an attendant drawing a thorn from an athlete's foot, and two scenes entitled "Wrestlers with their trainer in the palestra." Another, perhaps the first recorded instance of a trainer instructing the principles of fair play, is entitled "Trainer beating with his stick a youth who is gouging his opponent's eye." (1-4).

From the time the ancient Greeks pitched their tents on the plains of the Elis in the dim centuries of the past and brought together the young men of their land in the first of all Olympic games, until their modern revival in 1896 and down through recent times, the trainer has been an important factor in keeping the athlete in condition for top performance.

Through the years, the duties and qualifications of the trainers have changed in the same manner that the three R's of "readin, 'riting, and 'rithmetic" were changed to "Rockets, Radiation, and Rock and Roll." The crude methods of the old-time trainers have become a thing of the past. The day of "the rubber," the know-it-all, the jack-of-all-trades, and the master-of-none is over. After World War I, the athletic trainer as a specialist in the prevention of injury made his appearance in intercollegiate athletics. It was at this time, 1917, that Dr. S.E. Bilik published the first text devoted exclusively to athletic training and the treatment of athletic injuries (5,6). Other excellent publications have appeared since (7-18). (Numbers in parentheses refer to entries in bibliography at end of chapter).

The trainer today must have a sound understanding of the human body and be a keen and unbiased observer of the body in action. He must know a good deal about physiology, kinesiology, psychology, hygiene, massage, conditioning, therapeutic exercises, diet, and the various modalities of physical therapy. In addition, he is the "father confessor" of the squad.

The daily activities of the trainer are principally concerned with prevention of injury, treatment under medical direction, and rehabilitation.

Most trainers spend more time on prevention of injuries than is commonly believed by the average laymen or even by most school officials. It should be emphasized that treatment is only part of the trainer's duties and probably a less important part. The more injuries can be prevented, the fewer there will be to treat and rehabilitate. Since an injured athlete is of no value to his team, to his coach, or to himself, from an athletic standpoint, the greatest concern must be with prevention of the injury which causes his disability.

A most important phase of prevention is the physical and mental conditioning of the squad. It must be a vital part of the program. Bob Shelton of The University of Illinois, in an address before the Illinois Association for Health, Physical Education and Recreation, made the following statement: "Conditioning is more important than skill, because conditioning helps prevent injuries and the best halfback in the world is of no value sitting on the bench." (See Chapter III).

Many factors go into the field of prevention. As a part of prevention, no person should be permitted to practice or participate in any sport until he has successfully passed a thorough physical examination. The University of Oklahoma gives physical examinations on the so-called assembly-line technique. The team physician, doctors from the health center, and nurses begin physical examinations at the student health center at 7:30 a.m. on the day before fall practice starts. Each doctor takes a station. The athletes are given their record cards and they merely go from station to station. With the use of this technique, the entire varsity football squad completes its physical examinations in a relatively short period of time. (Approximately 2 1/2 hours).

Along this same line, it is advisable to have a physician on each bench at every contest. It may be necessary, in some localities, for various doctors to take turns; but, regardless of how it is done, a doctor can be rendering a service to his community by donating his services for a couple of afternoons or evenings each year.

Prevention also includes surveys of dressing rooms, shower rooms, playing fields, and equipment, to eliminate all possible hazards. An example is to make sure all helmets have the NOCSAE seal. Many schools spend most of their money and all of their time maintaining a so-called perfect game field - a field the spectators will see and the team will use four or five times a year. More important, the practice field, which is used as much in a week as the game field is in a season,

3

should be kept in A-1 condition at all times.

Good equipment is an important factor in the prevention of injuries. Some schools make the same mistake with equipment that they do with their practice field. They spend most of their budget for some gaudy, fancy game suit that is going to be worn only eight or ten times a year. It is my belief that a school should spend most of its money for the equipment that is worn daily - practice equipment. Although the budget is limited, no school should purchase large quantities of second-rate equipment, with which no player is properly protected. Instead, schools should purchase the best, even though the supply may be limited. Too much emphasis cannot be placed on a proper headgear. The modern lightweight headgear is effective, but does little good if the padding is worn out or if there is a crack in the headgear that prevents proper fitting. Once good equipment is supplied, the trainer and coach should insist that, in order to compete, the player wear the equipment that has been fitted to him.

At least a weekly check of each player's equipment should be made by the trainer or some other responsible person. Is the headgear too loose? Are the shoulder pads or hip pads broken? Are the pants so large that the thigh pads are slipping? How are the shoe cleats? The slipping of a thigh pad may result in a contusion (charley horse) which can keep a player inactive for the rest of the season.

From time to time during the season, it is necessary to improvise or purchase special equipment to protect a special injury. There are various commercial products which will allow special padding for bruised or separated shoulders and for protection of the iliac crest. It may be necessary to build up a pair of regular shoulder pads with sponge rubber or plastic to protect some of those special problems or even use a folded towel around the neck to prevent recurring neck strains or nerve contusions if a commercial product cannot be found. A physician should make the decision on which type of protection is appropriate for the neck area.

It is also necessary in fielding a team to do a considerable amount of preventive and protective taping. This will be discussed in subsequent chapters.

If the injury cannot be prevented, the first important step is early detection of its nature and degree. The best time to examine an athlete is at the time of the injury. Too often the injury is packed in ice or strapped until the next day. This is a dangerous practice. The trainer should work hand-in-hand with the team physician. They

4

should function as a team with the same set of rules and signals and the same objective - the complete rehabilitation of the player. Several conditions make the treatment of the athlete quite different from that of the ordinary patient. Dr. E.T. Smith of Houston, Texas, lists them as: (1) He is, or should be, strong, and in excellent physical condition. (2) He is young, and his healing and recuperative power is above average. (3) He has an incentive to get well, will cooperate to the fullest extent, and will tolerate early rehabilitative procedures. Because of these factors it is usually possible to get an athlete back into competition in a much shorter time than it is for an average workingman to return to his job.

Rehabilitative exercises should be started as soon as possible after an injury. In fact, it is advisable to continue exercising other portions of the body even though the injured part must of necessity be immobilized. It is much better to prevent atrophy than to relieve it. Obviously some exercises will be more suitable than others for a specific situation, and they must all be proportioned to the degree of disability of the individual player and gradually increased as he improves. It should be emphasized again that the player as a whole should be treated, not simply the injured part. It is only the unusual injury that will not permit active exercise of other parts of the body from the first day. *Recovery must be complete. One hundred per cent rehabilitation must be the goal.*

A related problem with which the trainer, coach, or team physician is confronted is the player who is afraid of injury. It is necessary to convince him that, if he gets himself in the proper condition, he will not be subject to injury. Pain is like a penny; it has two sides, organic and psychological.

The trainer is in a unique position to build confidence by convincing the player that, if he is in top physical condition, uses his equipment properly, is adequately warmed up, follows the coach's instructions precisely, and plays with "carefree abandon" and no hesitation, it is very unlikely that he will be hurt.

If confidence cannot be instilled and he remains "gun shy," he should be advised to drop out of the sport in the interest of his own safety.

It is encouraging to note that there are fewer serious injuries every year. This improvement can be explained in part by the fact that there are more qualified men in the field of conditioning, that better equipment has been designed and is being used, and that everyone is becoming increasingly concerned about the prevention of injuries. It has been said that, in the past, coaches were concerned about getting a team on the field, but that now they are vitally interested in keeping a team on the field. An adequate training program is one of the best means to accomplish this end.

It is a recognized fact that many schools cannot hire a full-time trainer. These schools should consider the hiring of a teacher-trainer, a qualified college graduate who has worked as an assistant trainer in college and who can also teach in the school system. It may even be possible in larger cities for two or three schools to hire a full-time trainer and establish a centralized training room in which all athletes can be cared for.

If neither of the above methods is feasible, perhaps each school can appoint a sincerely interested and responsible boy as a student trainer, and put him in charge of the training room, training equipment and first aid measures both on and off the field, but under the direct supervision of the coach. It would be advisable that the student trainer have no duties other than those connected with his training work. This student assistant will be able to perform numerous services which will give the coach more time in his already over-crowded schedule. To better educate student trainers in the principles of first aid, the Cramer Chemical Co., Gardner, Kansas, has inaugurated a summer correspondence course for all student trainers who are interested in enrolling.

Following are a few suggestions for student trainers (courtesy of the Cramer Chemical Co.):

1. Be the first man on the job and the last one to leave.
2. Keep your training room clean and neat, but don't spend time housekeeping when there are players needing attention.
3. Let the coach make and enforce rules. They are his responsibility, not yours.
4. Put your supplies away before going home at night. Get them out in the morning after you have put the room in order.
5. Find things to do in slack moments.
6. Prepare a "want list" of needed supplies. Make this a daily practice. It will be the coach's responsibility to order them if he feels they are necessary.
7. Always keep your first aid kit properly packed for field and trip use.
8. Keep your hands clean since they are your most important

tools. Keep your nails trimmed and clean under them before and after each day's work.

9. Dress neatly even though a regular uniform is not necessary. Prove you are worthy of the respect of the squad, and you will get it.

10. Ask the coach when you are in doubt.

11. Always be loyal to the coach. When things get tough, as they often do, prove that you are a part of the team.

12. Plan trips with the coach. Let him advise you on extra supplies that may be needed.

13. Don't get involved in local quarterback club discussions. Let the coach handle the news on player condition and prospects.

14. Do all you can to lessen the physical and mental load of the coach. He will be surprised at how well you can do it if you work at it properly.

15. Don't experiment with new methods until you have learned the merits and disadvantages of the old ones.

16. Do not try to classify an injury.

17. Do the best you can with what you have although you may not have as good a training room as your neighbor. Don't be a complainer or grumbler.

18. Don't have pets or favorites. Every star and scrub should rank equally in the training room, unless the coach instructs you differently. (Today's scrub may be next year's star).

19. Be thorough in order to save time. Close to 60% of your time will be spent preventing injury.

20. During practice or a game, pay particular attention to those you know have some sort of injury and check every player at half-time or as occasion permits.

21. Don't be guilty of letting a "little knowledge become dangerous." The coach and team or school physician must be responsible for the athlete's welfare.

22. Use your ears and eyes to improve the efficiency of your hands. In other words, read and observe what other trainers and coaches are doing.

If possible a physician should be available at all contests. If each school were to provide a physician at all of its home contests, it would not be necessary for the physicians to travel with the visiting team.

References

1. Thorwaldsen Museum, Copenhagen, No. 112, and Museum

fur antike Kleinhunst, Munich, N. 2344.

2. Altes Museum, Berlin, No. 2180.

3. Altes Museum, Berlin, No. 2159.

4. Metropolitan Museum of Art, *Greek Athletics* (3rd ed.), New York, 1933. Plandome Press.

5. Bilik, S.E., *The Trainers' Bible* (8th revised ed.), New York 1947. T. J. Reed Co.

6. Bilik, S.E., *Athletic Training and the Treatment of Athletic Injuries* (3rd ed.), New York, 1923. Atsco Press.

7. Cramer, F., Boughton, L.L. and Cramer, C., *A Training Room Manual*, Gardner, Kansas, 1944. Cramer Co.

8. Dolan, J.P., *Treatment and Prevention of Athletic Injuries* (1st ed.), Danville, IL, 1955. Interstate Co.

9. Thorndike, A., *Athletic Injuries, Prevention, Diagnosis and Treatment* (3rd ed.), Philadelphia, 1948. Lea & Febiger.

10. Morehouse, L.F. and Rasch, P.J., *Scientific Basis of Athletic Training* (1st ed.), Philadelphia, 1958. W.B. Saunders Co.

11. Hopenfeld, Stanley, *Physical Examination of the Spine and Extremities,* Appleton-Century-Crofts. Copyright 1976.

12. Klafs, Carl E., and Arnheim, Daniel D., *Modern Principles of Athletic Training* (2nd ed.), The C.V. Mosby Co., 1969.

13. Burnett, R., Personal Communication

14. Secretary's report. Second annual convention and clinic of the National Athletic Trainer's Association, Kansas City, MO, June 1951.

15. O'Donoghue, D.H., and Rawlinson, K., *The Prevention and Treatment of Athletic Injuries,* J. Oklahoma M.A., 49: 219-221, 255-258, 263-264, 302-306, 310, 1956.

16. Quigley, T.B., Cox, J., and Murphy, J., *Protective Wrapping for the Ankle,* J.A.M.A. 132: 924, 1946.

17. Hanley, D.F., Personal Communication

18. Rawlinson, K.B., *Symposium on Sports Injuries,* American Journal of Surgery, 98: 337, 1959.

II

The Training Room

THE TRAINING ROOM

It is a known fact that not every school can have an ideal training room, but every school can have a clean training room.

Cleanliness Must Be The Keynote

It is extremely difficult to specify the actual equipment and supplies as there is great difference in the size of schools, their budgets, and their needs. Any equipment and supplies purchased should be approved by the team physician. The trainer should work hand-in-hand with him and use nothing of which he does not approve. He should make the best of what he has, hoping that perhaps sometime in the future the room can be enlarged and more equipment added. The most important thing in the training room is the person who is in charge of the operation - the trainer himself.

Following are some considerations which are necessary in setting up the training room:

A. Location
1. Separate quarters - away from dressing room and coaches' office, but relatively close for easy access by the athletes.
2. Bathroom near training room.
3. Proximity to exercise and game area.
B. General Plan
1. A light, pleasant color paint (waterproof and washable).
2. Good ventilation, outlet fans.
3. Adequate heat and cooling.
4. Adequate fluorescent overhead lighting.
5. Sufficient electrical outlets at least 4' above floor.
6. If possible, a carpet floor. Linoleum or tile floor may be used.
7. Telephone (for doctors and trainer only).
8. If only one room is available, one large enough to contain at least:
a. Training tables (to accommodate 1-20 athletes). Size - 74'' x 24'' x 30'' to 34''.
b. Taping tables (to accommodate 1-20 athletes). Size - 36'' x 24'' x 34''
c. Sink with hot and cold water.

      d.   Essential physical therapy equipment (under equipment).

      e.   Area for rehabilitation equipment (under equipment).

      f.   Desk for trainer and physician.

      g.   File for records.

      h.   Shelves in office area.

      i.   Freezer.

      j.   Table for sterilizer and supplies.

      k.   Chairs.

      l.   Trash containers.

   9. If more than one room is available, the following items are helpful:

      a.   Physical therapy and rehabilitation room.

      b.   Office for trainer and physician, with examination table.

      c.   Ice whirlpool area.

      d.   X-ray room.

      e.   Bulletin board and area for anatomy charts.

C. Equipment

   1. Physical Therapy

      a.   Whirlpool bath (at least one large and one small) that includes seating in or around whirlpool.

      b.   Diathermy.

      c.   Steam pack unit.

      d.   Ultra sound

      e.   Paraffin bath.

      f.   Hand vibrator.

   2. Rehabilitation Equipment

      a.   Progressive resistance - exercise equipment (weights for various extremities, stationary bicycle, shoulder wheel, etc.).

      b.   Traction unit.

      c.   Hanging bar (shoulders, etc.).

   3. Medical equipment and trainers

      a.   Stretchers (on field).

      b.   Crutches (adjustable) and canes.

      c.   Air splints (leg, ankle, arm, hand, etc.).

      d.   Oxygen unit.

      e.   Magnifying glass.

        f.   Plastic ice bags.

        g.   Electric hair clippers and razors.

        h.   Bandage scissors.

        i.   Tape cutters.

        j.   Ankle wrap roller.

        k.   Special items requested by the team physician.
- 1. Surgical instruments and sutures.
- 2. Syringes and needles.

        l.   Portable training table.

        m. Airway.

        n.   Oral screw, tongue forceps, ammonia capsules (use with caution).

D. Supplies (partial listing)

  1. Sterile dressings
- a. Gauze pads (2x2, 3x3, 4x4).
- b. Band-aids.
- c. Stretch gauze.

  2. Non-sterile dressings
- a. Gauze roll bandage (1'', 2'', 3'').
- b. Absorbent cotton roll.
- c. Gauze pads (2'' x 2'', 3'' x 3'', 4'' x 4'').
- d. Ankle wraps (72 yard roll to be cut to desired length, usually 96'' length).
- e. Elastic bandage (2'', 3'', 4'' and 6'').
- f. Triangular bandage.

  3. Adhesive Tape
- a. Regular with zinc oxide (1/2'', 1'', 1 1/2'', 2'').
- b. Elastic (2'', and 3'').
- c. Moleskin.

  4. Ointments
- a. Analgesic balm (various strengths).
- b. Cold cream.
- c. Foot ointments for athletes foot, etc.
- d. Ointments for abrasions and turf burns.
- e. Black sun glare cream.
- f. Antibiotic ointment.
- g. Petroleum jelly.
- h. Zinc oxide.
- i. Antibiotics.
- j. Tinactin.

5. Padding
    a. Felt (3/8'', 1/4'').
    b. Plastic.
    c. Foam rubber for special pads.
    d. Corn pads.
    e. Bruise pads.
    f. Foot pads.
6. Powders
    a. Foot and body powder.
    b. Epsom salts.
    c. Rosin.
7. Solutions
    a. Alcohol diluted to 70% strength.
    b. Isopropyl alcohol.
    c. Various rub down lotions.
    d. Athletes foot spray or liquid.
    e. Tape adherent (spray and liquid).
    f. Lotion for hives and rashes.
    g. Oil of clove.
    h. Cough syrup.
    i. Eye wash.
    j. Tape remover.
    k. Pepto-Bismol.
    l. Kaopectate.
    m. Hydrogen peroxide.
    n. Throat gargle (or salt).
8. Tablets
    a. Aspirin 5 gr.
    b. Cold capsules (various types).
    c. Sugar tablets.
    d. Anti-acid tablets for stomach.
    e. Various vitamins (multiple, etc.).
9. Miscellaneous
    a. Cotton tip applicators.
    b. Tongue depressors.
    c. Elastic thigh caps (sleeves).
    d. Elastic knee caps (sleeves).
    e. Cast material.
    f. Rib belts (various sizes).
    g. Mouth pieces.

      h.   Atomizers.

      i.   Blankets.

      j.   Fire extinguishers.

      k.   Back and neck boards.

      l.   Heel cups.

      m.   Toothache wax.

10.   Other equipment and supplies as suggested by physician.

The whirlpool bath is one of the most popular physical therapeutic devices used today. It can be used in treating practically any type of injury: sprains, strains, contusions, bone injuries, post fractures, bursitis, circulatory disturbances, tendonitis, painful joints, scar tissue, nerve injuries, adhesions, arthritis, etc. - that is, if it is used properly.

Several factors influence the length of time for each treatment. In treatment of an extremity, the average length of time is twenty minutes; if the patient is submerged to the hips, the average time is 12-15 minutes; if the entire body is submerged, the treatment time should be from 5-10 minutes. Anyone in the whirlpool should be closely watched by a trainer.

The temperature of the water is also a variable in determining the length of time one is to be in the whirlpool.

Insofar as water temperature is concerned, the more acute the injury, the lower the intensity of heat; heat will cause swelling to an injured area. The following rules in regard to the water temperature in pools seem to work well:

New injury or injury with swelling - under 100°

Injury at least 3-4 days old (little swelling) - 100° - 103°

Old, chronic injury - 103° - 106°

As a safety precaution, the whirlpool should be well grounded by school electricians and checked on a regular basis. It should also have a working thermometer. Sapping of an individual's strength is related to the length of treatment and temperature of the water. The athlete should be observed closely after a treatment because of a tendency of some to become light-headed.

The freezer and then the whirlpool are often the first pieces of therapy equipment which should be placed in the training room.

Many schools cannot afford some of the above therapeutic equipment. However, it is possible to improvise and make therapy equipment which will aid in the treatment of athletic injuries. Some of the home-made equpiment or relatively inexpensive equipment which have proven of value are:

1. Contrast baths - very effective in stimulating circulation to the extremities. Fill one bucket or large trash container with hot water (103° - 106°) and one with cold water (45° - 50°). Alternately submerge the extremity into the buckets, starting with the hot and ending with hot if there is no swelling. Where there is swelling, end with cold. The ratio will vary. Hot-to-cold ratio (in minutes): 10-1, 6-4, 5-3, 3-1, (This is best for most injuries).

2. Shower - adjust the nozzle so that there is a forceful, direct spray, especially good on the neck, shoulders and back.

3. Hot towels.

4. Hot-tub soaking.

5. Hot water bottle.

6. Ice.

7. Water-cooling box.

8. Steam packs (purchase own heating unit.) (Hydro collator).

9. Paraffin bath. Use three parts of paraffin (jelly wax) to one part of vaseline in a homemade container.

10. Ice massage - fill styrofoam cup with water and freeze. Very inexpensive and the most commonly used type of therapy.

11. Steam bath.

III

Conditioning Athletes' Bodies

For top performance, body conditioning is absolutely necessary. A conditioned body is less susceptible to injuries. Conditioning affects:

1. Ability to play.
2. Mental attitude.
3. Determination.
4. Teamwork.
5. Spirit.

Many fail to make the team because they do not have the desire. They will not pay the price to get themselves into shape both physically and mentally. Mental conditioning is a phase often overlooked, but it is vital. Many athletes do not think it is important, but it goes hand-in-hand with physical conditioning. If an athlete is going to be great, he must have both.

Former Oklahoma Coach, Bud Wilkinson, has often made the statement that the difference between a champion and a fellow who plays well is:

1. The fellow who slows up a little ten yards from the end of a wind sprint (and this is the human trait) is lazy, takes the easy way out.

2. The champion is a man who can finish. He has no folding point.

Basic Principles of Running

An important phase of conditioning is running. Every athlete should learn how to run correctly. Anyone can be taught to run a little faster, if he has the desire. Following are a few suggestions:

1. Relax. The body must be supple to attain best performance.
2. Run on balls of feet.
3. Point the toes straight ahead. You lose at least one half inch on each step if the toes are not straight ahead.
4. Run in a straight line. It is the shortest distance between two points.
5. Develop your proper stride. The average stride is the height of your body. Lengthen your stride as much as possible, but do not overstride. An overstride is worse than an understride.
6. Observe the correct running angle: body leaning; head up; ankles, hips, shoulders and head in a straight line. Do not bend backward. You should be in the proper running angle and with the proper stride 12-15 yards from the starting point.

7. Move opposite arm and leg is unison. Keep arm relaxed and shoot uppercuts to height of shoulder and not beyond center of body. Bring arm back so hand does not go beyond crest of hip, a relaxed piston-like movement.

NOTE:

Short sprints develop speed.

Distance;running develops endurance.

Running in circles and figure eights strengthens ankles, knees, hips, and backs.

Summer Conditioning for High School Athletes

Most trainers believe that a high school athlete needs even more incentive to carry on a summer conditioning program than a college athlete. Following is a summer, off-season conditioning plan that can be inaugurated in any high school.

A. Personal letters to the boys.

B. Physical examination.

C. Gradual start to reach peak in August.

D. A plan or chart for boys to follow.

    1. Conditioning exercises.

    2. Running (6:30 mile or its equivalent).

    3. Wind sprints.

    4. Step climb, forward and backward.

    5. Specific rehabilitation exercises.

    6. Temperate living.

        a. Sleep — "the great restorer" — a minimum of nine hours. Two hours before midnight is better than four after.

        b. Good diet. (See Chapter 6).

        c. No intoxicants. The A.M.A. has stated that "alcohol is a detriment to the human organism. Its use in therapeutics, as a tonic, food, or stimulant has no scientific value. It attacks the central nervous system. It is not a food; it is a poison."

        d. No smoking. Nowhere is there any medical evidence that smoking improves an athlete's ability. It actually slows him up. Nicotine is a poison. If one smokes a pack of cigarettes a day for a week, he inhales 400 mg. of nicotine, which in a single injection would kill him instantly.

e. No drugs. The United States Olympic Committee has recently ruled that any competitor who uses drugs, stimulants, or other substances known as ''dope'' for any purpose will be disqualified.

A good pre-season conditioning program, if rehabilitation work is year round, may be as follows:

Early Suggestions to the Athlete

Run early mornings or late in the evening to avoid the *heat* of the day.

Run with a teammate of your own ability.

Wear loose-fitting clothing and good quality jogging shoes.

Stage I — Long Distance — (Cross-Country Running)

June 2 — July 4

Long distance training is continuous running at a slow speed with a minimum distance of 3 miles a day. The speed of your run will probably vary between 8-10 minutes per mile.

Objectives of Long distance Running

1. Build endurance and stamina.
2. Strengthen and make supple the muscles and connective fibers.
3. Improve the cardiovascular system (heart, veins, and arteries).

Long Distance Program

1. Have an exact distance measured off — high school track, cross-country course, road mileage measured in your car, etc.
2. Starting June 2, run 3 miles a day, 3 days a week (example Monday, Wednesday, and Friday) through June 21.
3. Starting June 22, run 5 days a week through July 4.
4. If you have to stop and walk during run, do not count the distance walked as part of the 3 miles.
5. Continue to do your weight-lifting exercises and football drills.

Stage II — Interval and Speed Running

July 7 — August 15

Interval Running

This is repeated short-distance speed work with stretches of slower running used for recovery (Example: Run 1 — Jog 1).

The main incentive is that it is more demanding than long-distance running.

Speed Running

These are short sprints usually done at 3/4 of maximum speed. In longer distance sprinting, start slow and increase your pace over the latter part of the sprint.

Objectives.

1. Improve your ability to accelerate.
2. Enable you to run faster.
3. Increase in overall conditioning.

A. Warm Up (Every Day)
   1. Flexibility exercises
   2. Light jog 3/4 mile
   3. More flexibility exercises
   4. Stride 10-40 yards with **high** knee action

B. Monday-Wednesday (Interval Days)
   1. Do this on a measured track (preferably on 440 track) and start on July 10.
   2. Run eight-440 yard runs in approximately **75** to **80** seconds.
   3. After each 440, jog slowly around another 440. You will run 8-440's and jog slowly 8-440's.

C. Tuesday-Thursday (Speed Days)
   Sprints
   4-50 yd. — last 20 yds. at 3/4 speed. Stress form. Walk back to start.
   6-75 yd. — last 25 yds. at 3/4 speed. Stress form. Walk back to start
   5-110 yd. — last 30 yds. at 3/4 speed. Strees form. Walk back to start.
   3-150 yd. — last 35 yds. at 3/4 speed. Stress form. Walk back to start.

2-220 yd. — first 110 yds. slow, pick up the last 110 yds. Stress form.

1-330 yd. — first 220 yds. slow, pick up the last 110 yds. Stress form.

D. Friday — Test Day (Stage III) or a Monday-Wednesday workout.

E. Saturday
   1. 3 mile long-distance run.

Stage III — Test

1. Test run only on **Friday**.
2. Test run a series of 110 yard runs taking approximately 17 seconds.
3. Rest 30 seconds between runs.
4. Do this on a measured football field or track. Have someone to time you.
5. Each week try to increase your number of repetitions. (18 repetitions is reasonably good. 28 repetitions is outstanding.)
6. Do not use test as a daily workout.
7. Increase your repetitions and decrease the time over the 110 yd urse so that you **know** you are getting stronger and faster. Beginning July 7 you will receive a running card in the mail each week. You will record your results from the test day each Friday.

SUMMER WEIGHT-TRAINING PROGRAM

Weight training is concerned with the development of increased physical capacity — that is, greater muscular endurance, greater strength, increased speed of movement and greater power.

Objective of Our Weight Program

The purpose of this out-of-season (summer) weight-training program is to develop **strength** and **power**. It is imperative for the football player to overcome the resistance of an opposing player and to exert force when needed by using the explosive power built by progressive weight-training exercise. Only with hard work will the player accomplish his goal.

Warm-Up (This is just as important as the workout itself and requires a positive attitude.)

1. Be consistent with your day-to-day warm-up. Do all forms of strenuous exercise with a systematic warm-up; **this includes weight-training!** Your muscles will not perform near a maximum level of contraction unless "warmed-up." Prevent strains of muscles, and other related problems — tendonitis, etc.

2. Prior to each workout, do the following:
A. Spend 15-20 minutes on **slow** and **deliberate** stretching and calisthenics.
B. Run in a light, slow, deliberate manner. Concentrate on your activity.
C. Warm-up each muscle group by lifting a few light weights. Go through the entire routine lightly. (Break a sweat.)

The Summer Program — Free Weights

1. Work-out three times a week, with a day's rest between (Example: Monday, Wednesday, and Friday or Tuesday, Thursday, and Saturday). Do no over-tax your body by lifting every day.
2. Don't drag out your workouts. Go about your business deliberately with positive goals. Remember that mental attitude is the difference when the competition is tough.
3. **Do all sets to complete exhaustion to where you cannot lift another weight.**
4. Use for the first two days of your workout (Monday & Wednesday) a weight that is 80-90% of your maximum at that particular exercise.
5. On the third day use a weight that is 50-75% of your maximum at that particular exercise.
6. Allow 2-4 minutes rest between sets (allow time for recovery).
7. Do the number of sets and repetitions prescribed.
8. Add weight as you progress and increase in strength.

FREE WEIGHT WORK-OUT PROGRAM

EXERCISE	REPETITIONS SETS (Mon-Wed) *		REPETITIONS SETS (Friday) *		DEVELOPMENT
Bench Press (shoulder width)	3-6	4	10-15	2	Chest, Shoulders
Power cleans	3-6	4	10-15	3	Shoulders, Back, Arms
Dead Lift (Olympic style) & Shrug	3-6	4	10-15	2	Back, Shoulders
Squats (one quarter)	3-6	4	10-15	3	Legs, Hips
Power Curls (Front)	3-6	3	10-15	2	Arms
Leg Curls (Machine)	8-10	3	12-20	2	Legs (Hamstrings)
Leg Extensors (Machine)	8-10	3	12-20	2	Legs (Quadriceps)
Sit-Ups (Bent Legged)	25	3	40	2	Abdominal Area

— Add weight as you progress

*Work-outs can be set up on a Monday-Wednesday-Friday or Tuesday-Thursday-Saturday basis.

THE INGREDIENTS OF GREATNESS

As a part of athletes' mental conditioning, the following qualities and applications can be posted in the training room.

C — oncentration
H — eart
A — ttitude
M — odesty
P — ractice
S — acrifice

IV

Practice Routines

The time spent on the practice field will vary according to such factors as weather conditions, experience of squad, day of the week. One cannot set down any hard and fast rule, but the tendency is to practice too long, and with too much scrimmage. Many teams leave Saturday's game on the practice field.

Following is a chart of a possible program for practice sessions:

TIME TO BE SPENT ON PRACTICE FIELD

	Average Time
Prior to Week of Opening Game	1:39
Week Prior to Opening Game	1:02
Week Prior to Open Date	1:14
Week Prior to Second Game	1:07
Week Prior to Third Game	1:09
Week Prior to Fourth Game	1:04
Week Prior to Fifth Game	1:05
Week Prior to Sixth Game	:50
Week Prior to Seventh Game	1:13
Week Prior to Eighth Game	1:11
Week Prior to Ninth Game	:58
Week Prior to Tenth Game	:59
Prior to Leaving for Final Game	1:13

Many people believe that a light practice routine will not work in high school. This is not always accurate at Ada High School in Oklahoma. In one of the toughest conferences in the country, Ada won six out of eight state championships and had a record of 90 victories and seven losses from 1950 through 1958. Their successful records continued through the 60's and 70's.

In an article written by Ray Soldan and published in *The Daily Oklahoman* on September 18, 1955, he explains the Ada theory as follows:

The Ada Cougars, mythical state champions in 1954, are a prime example of a new theory in coaching: that you don't have to "rough it up" in practice to turn out a good football team.

Elvan George, Ada's veteran coach (now head coach at East Central College) limits his charges to conditioning drills, dummy scrimmages, and plenty of individual instruction. The Cougars never have game condition scrimmages and do no tackling. The only contact work the club engages in is a little hitting among the linemen.

"We don't even have practice pants," George said. "We work out in shorts all the time. The only regulation garb we wear in practices is shoulder pads and helmets and we wear those only for the feel of the equipment. Our linemen wear jerseys, but our backs just don T-shirts to keep the shoulder pads from flapping."

The highly-successful Ada coach revealed that he has been experimenting with the unique practice method for three years. The club used the system 100 percent one year for the first time and rolled triumphantly through an 11-game schedule.

What are the merits of the no-contact system? George cites the following:

1. There is little chance for practice injuries. We suffered none last year.

2. We can do considerably more running and agility work.

3. We feel it makes our timing better.

4. Every kid has to hustle because in our system of individual drills the coaches can see exactly what each boy is doing. In scrimmage sessions, you often see some loafing.

5. We get an extra hour of practice a week on most teams because we work an hour and a half every Thursday. We can do it since we don't need the time to recuperate.

What are the disadvantages? "There no doubt are some," George commented, "but we're sold on our system."

PRACTICE ROUTINES

In 1959, under coach Craig McBroom, Ada won 11 and lost 2, then won the state championship. Mr. McBroom is a firm believer in Mr. George's practice policies, and he recently told me that in 1957 and 1958, when he coached at the Ada Junior High School, although his teams scrimmaged only four times in the two years they were not scored against in 1958.

Mr. McBroom states, "During the two-a-day practice sessions at Oklahoma, we practice at 7:00 a.m. and again at 4:00 p.m. Since we do not eat breakfast until after the morning workout, we have available at the dressing room orange juice (with honey) to drink. After much experimenting, it was found the boys prefer this juice to any other.

"During the practice sessions (before the cool weather) we take a 5-minute break midway through the afternoon session and give the boys a saline solution to help replenish the salt lost during practice and as an aid in quenching the boys' thirst."

V

The Game Weekend

A game weekend is the same whether a team is playing at home or away. On Fridays most teams have a short practice in sweatsuits (the average time about 17-20 minutes for each practice). Friday practices average about 22 minutes. After practice the athletes take a refreshing shower.

At 6:30 p.m. comes the Friday evening meal. Refer to Chapter VI for meal plan.

After dinner the men usually go to a movie as a group. All must be in their rooms by 10:00 p.m. and lights out by 10:30 p.m.

For a 1:30 p.m. game the squad is awakened at 8:45 a.m. for the 9:30 a.m. pre-game meal. The meal is compulsory for all, even coaches. The pre-game meal consists of a very nutritious diet (Refer to Chapter VI to see a typical pre-game meal).

Large glass of orange juice
Choice of dry cereal, enough milk to moisten
8 oz. filet mignon with sauces
Two loosely scrambled eggs
Toast, butter, honey
Tea or coffee

Following breakfast comes a squad meeting at which time players and trainers begin taping all the ankles.

Pre-Game Nervousness

Some of the athletes have diet peculiarities. For example, some cannot digest orange juice, eggs, or milk. In this event, the food which causes the digestive problem is eliminated. If it is just a pre-game nervous stomach, Tittralac, Pepto-Bismol, Kaopectate, or cracked ice often brings relief.

Rain Preparation

Clear shoe wax (polish) is acceptable treatment for wet hands or forearm. The student-trainer should take it on field at time-outs. Rosin or any tape adherent is acceptable. Tape on the ankles (on socks), plenty of thick paste (firm grip of some sort) are useful to the athlete.

Pre-game Equipment Preparations

Arrange for a doctor to be on the bench and an ambulance to be at the field; provide stretchers, oxygen, ice, necessary medications and protective equipment. An orthopedic surgeon should be on the bench at all times.

Preparations for Visiting Team

Provide a manager (or student-trainer) to run errands; a well-lighted training room with appropriate number of taping tables; a stretcher on their bench; medical care if they do not have a physician with them; instructions on where the ambulance is located; towels; water; equipment that they may have forgotten; soft drinks or fruit if they so desire.

Care of Boys on Sidelines and at Time-Outs

You should watch the field at all times. If for any reason you have to take your eyes off the field, you should assign one of your assistants to watch and to call you immediately if there is an injury. Watch every play as this can give a definite clue as to what type of injury to expect. Assign one assistant to sponge off and check for injuries all boys coming out of the game and one assistant to provide them with water. At time-outs assign one assistant to take water (in a plastic squirt-bottle) and towels on the field. You should also go on the field to check injuries and fatigue.

Half-time Procedures

Check all injuries while the assistants check equipment and provide the boys with cola drinks, ice bags, or whatever is needed. You do not need to tell the boys how much to drink at the half. Leave that up to them.

Following the game away from home, on board the plane have available as much orange juice as the players wish. The meal on the plane may consist of the following:

Fruit Cup
Salad
1/2 Fried Chicken
Mashed Potatoes
Vegetables
Roll, butter

Ice Cream (all they want)
Milk (all they want)

Following home games, have cola drinks in the dressing room. After the boys are dressed they go to the training table where they have a meal similar to the one described above (on plane).

Sunday Morning Routine

It is a good idea to have the training room open from 9:30 a.m. to 10:30 a.m. and have every boy who played on Saturday report for treatment if injured. At that time the team physician should be available to examine the injuries.

Sunday Afternoon Routine

Squad has meetings and running sessions are helpful. Training room may be open from 2:30 p.m. to 3:30 p.m. for treatments.

Monday-Friday Routine

Have the training room open from 8:00 a.m. — 12:00 noon and from 1:30 p.m. to the end of practice.

VI

The Athlete's Diet

THE ATHLETE'S DIET

A wholesome diet for an athlete should be composed of a variety of good foods. There is no magic pill, wonder food, or surefire formula which will make one a better athlete, but a proper diet will help to keep one at his best.

One should start every day with a good, solid, substantial breakfast (fruit or fruit juice, cereal, eggs, ham or bacon, toast and beverage). Breakfast is the foundation for the day, and no building or day is any better than its foundation. The breakfast, without a doubt the most important meal of the day, should include at least 1/3 of the daily calorie intake.

Training Table

For breakfast, some teams receive a choice of bacon (fried) or grilled ham, eggs (fried, scrambled, or poached if requested), gravy, hot cereal (oatmeal, malt-o-meal, hominy grits), toast (white, wheat, rye), and sweet rolls (home-made). For variety, there are sometimes hot biscuits, French toast, hot cakes, cinnamon toast, doughnuts, and hash brown potatoes. Dry cereals are also available (not many sugar-coated) and fresh fruit, canned fruit, and fruit juices of various varieties.

Most diets include **lots** of beef. Filler is never added to any ground beef. There usually are two kinds of meat and roast beef is kept in the warmer for the boys to help themselves. Coaches and trainers do not count calories. The individual player himself will know whether he has to gain or lose.

There should be three or more vegetables a day for lunch and dinner (the color of the vegetable is important) in addition to some type of potatoes (buttered, chunk fried, French fried, mashed, potato salad, potato chips) or onion rings. Breads consist of white, rye, wheat, homemade, corn muffins, gingerbread, or banana bread. For dessert, cakes, cobblers, fruit pies, cream pies, canned fruit, and ice cream are suitable. Ice cream may be available at all times in the dining hall.

On the training table, there should always be tea (hot or cold), coffee, milk (homogenized and chocolate), fruit punch (or lemonade), and grape drink. Also important are oleo, jelly, honey, peanut butter and a honey-butter.

Suggestions for Losing Weight

1. Reduce only under medical supervision.
2. Do not skip meals.
3. Eat well balanced meals consisting of 1500 to 1800 calories per day.
4. Eat nothing between meals or before bedtime.
5. Continue with daily activity — exercise.
6. Avoid sweets.
7. Weigh at the same time each day, preferably upon arising.
8. Substitute lemon juice or vinegar for salad dressings.

Dr. Dale Thomas from Oregon State, states, "Reducing is a matter of calorie intake and energy output. If you burn up more calories exercising, working out, competing, than you consume you will lose weight. Scientists as a rule of thumb in calculating reducing diets, estimate that a deficit of 3500 calories will be required to affect a loss of one pound. If an athlete is using 3800 calories per day and eats 2000, he can expect to lose about 1/2 pound."

SAMPLE OF AN APPROXIMATE 1,200 CALORIE DIET (Do not diet without a doctor's permission).

Breakfast

Tomato juice, 1/2 cup	25	calories
Corn flakes, 1 cup	80	
Skim milk to moisten	20	
2 eggs, boiled or poached	140	
1 strip of crisp bacon 4" x 1"	30	
Bread, 1 slice	70	
Tea or coffee, black	00	
(Same as a piece of pie)	365	

Lunch

Hamburger Patty, Lean 1/5 lb	250	calories
Green beans, canned, 1/2 cup	20	
Cantaloupe, 1/2	40	
Skimmed milk, 8 0z.	85	
Bread, 1 slice	70	
(Approximately the same as 8 oz. chocolate milk)	465	

Dinner

Veal cutlet (average)	250	calories
Tomatoes, 1/2 cup (canned or fresh)	20	
Mixed green salad, light oil	30	
Grapefruit, 1/2	45	
Skimmed milk, 8 0z.	85	
Bread, 1/2 slice	35	
(Approximately the same as a hot dog)	465	

Sample of an 1800 Calorie Diet

Depending on certain variables this diet may cause some athletes to gain weight and others to lose weight. (Do not diet without doctor's permission).

1800 Calorie Reduction Diet

Meal Plan

Breakfast	Lunch	Supper
1 serv. fruit or juice	3 oz. meat	3 oz. meat
1 serv. meat or egg	3 bread or equiv.	3 bread or equiv.
2 bread or cereal	2 vegetables	2 vegetables
2 fat	2 fat	2 fat
1 c. skim milk	1 fresh fruit	2 fresh fruit
	1 c. skim milk	1 c. skim milk

Monday

1/2 c. orange jc.	3 oz. FF spiced ham	3 oz. FF roast beef
1 FF egg	1/2 c. pinto beans	(no gravy)
3/4 c. dry cereal	1/2 c. FF spinach	1/2 c. mashed potatoes
(unsweetened)	sliced tomatoes,	1/2 c. FF mix. veg.
1 buttered toast	as desired	Lettuce/1 Tb. dress.

1 slice bacon
1 c. skim milk

2 small pieces cornbread
2 pats oleo
1 serv. fresh fruit
1 c. skim milk

2 rolls 1 oleo
2 fresh fruit
1 c. skim milk

Tuesday

1 med. orange
1 FF Egg
3/4 c. dry cereal
1 bu. toast
1 bacon
1 c. skim milk

1 c. vegetable soup
3/4 c. cottage cheese
   or 3 oz. FF roast beef
Shred. lettuce / 1 Tb. Dr.
10 saltines 2 oleo
1 fresh fruit
1 c. skim milk

3 oz. FF t-bone
1 med. bk. potato
1/2 c. FF green peas
Tossed salad, vinegar
2 rolls 2 oleo
2 fresh fruit
1 c. skim milk

Wednesday

1/2 Banana
3/4 c. dry cereal
1 oz. ham
1 bu. toast
1 c. skim milk

1 c. tomato soup
3 oz. FF bk. chicken
Lettuce, 1 Tb. Dress.
5 saltines 1 oleo
1 fresh fruit
1 c. skim milk

3 oz. FF ham
1 small bk. potato
1/2 c FF green beans
2 rolls 2 oleo
2 fresh fruit
1 c. skim milk

Thursday

1/2 c. orange juice
1 FF egg
2 bu. toast
1 c. skim milk

2 sli. lunch meat
   & 1 oz. cheese
2 sli. bread
2 tsp. may, mustard
Lettuce and tomato
1 bk. Apple, no sugar
1 c. skim milk

3 oz. FF steak
1/2 c. msh. potato
1/2 c. FF gr. peas
Lettuce, 1 TB. dr.
2 rolls 2 oleo
2 fresh fruit
1 c. skim milk

Friday

1/2 c. grapefruit jc.
1 FF egg
3/4 c. dry cereal
1 bu. toast
1 bacon
1 c. skim milk

3 oz. FF bk. catfish
   or 3 oz. FF beef
1/2 c. macaroni & cheese
1/2 c. FF cooked cabbage
Lettuce, 1 TB. dr.
2 rolls 1 oleo
1 fresh fruit
1 c. skim milk

3 oz. FF liver or beef
1/2 c. FF potatoes
1/2 c. FF cooked veg.
Tossed Salad, 1 Tb. dr.
2 rolls, 2 oleo
2 fresh fruit
1 c. skim milk

Saturday

1/2 c. orange jc.
1 oz. sausage
3/4 c. dry cereal
1 dry toast
1 c. skim milk

3 oz. FF roast beef
1/2 c. msh. potato
1/2 c. FF gr. beans
Tossed salad, vinegar
1 fresh fruit
1 c. skim milk

3 oz. FF turkey
1/4 c. bk. beans
1/2 c. cooked veg.
Sliced tomatoes
2 fresh fruit
1 c. skim milk

37

Sunday

1/2 c. gfrt. jc.	3 oz. FF bk. chicken	Cheeseburger with
1 FF egg	1/2 C. msh. potatoes	2 tsp. mayo, mustard,
3/4 c. dry cereal	1/2 c. FF gr. peas	Lettuce & tomato, Dill
1 bu. toast	Tossed salad, 1 TB. dr.	pickles
1 bacon	2 rolls 1 oleo	Tossed salad, vinegar
1 c. skim milk	1 fresh fruit	2 fresh fruit
	1 c. skim milk	1 c. skim milk

Suggestions for Gaining Weight

1. Have a physical examination.
2. Avoid undue fatigue, take moderate exercise, relax.
3. Eat high-calorie food slowly and often — mid-morning, mid-afternoon, and bed time.
4. Get more sleep and take mid-afternoon naps.
5. Reverse procedure listed under "Suggestions for Losing Weight."

Pre-Competition Meal

There are many theories as to what an athlete should eat, pre-game meal or otherwise. There is no one rule that dictates what an athlete should eat or whether he should eat. A dedicated athlete can usually be relied upon to use good judgment in general training habits.

Over the years the traditional pre-game meal has consisted primarily of high protein foods, i.e., steak and eggs. Because of the athletes' nervous stomach, a few would have some digestion problems with this diet because it takes somewhat longer to digest. A pre-game meal consisting of mainly carbohydrates i.e., pancakes, bread, or even spaghetti (not highly seasoned) is now recommended because the carbohydrates will provide the quickest and most efficient source of energy and have neither the slow gastric emptying problem of the fats nor the dehydrating tendency of protein.

A Pre-Game Meal May Contain:

Friday — Dinner
Fruit cup (fresh)

Tossed green salad (Thousand Island Dressing)
12-oz. tenderloin steak (well done)
Baked potato (with butter and/or sour cream)
Peas and carrots
Rolls and butter
Honey (on table in dishes)
Ice cream and cookies
Pint of milk
Condiments on tables

Saturday — Game Day — Breakfast
Large glass orange juice
Choice of cereal (milk for cereal, half & half in pitchers)
Two fresh eggs softly scrambled
10-oz. tenderloin steak (well done)
Two slices dry toast
Two pats butter
Honey (on table in dishes)
Tea or coffee
Condiments on tables

Breakfast — (Available to any athlete)
Same menu as above breakfast except substitute **4 large pancakes**
for the tenderloin steak.

VII

*Types of Injuries and
Their General Treatment*

TYPES OF INJURIES AND THEIR GENERAL TREATMENT

In diagnosing an injury, the trainer should take into consideration:
1. What he sees.
2. What he hears.
3. What he feels.
4. Answers to questions (History).
5. Comparison - Deformity?
6. Reason and common sense.

Types of Injuries - (Seven true injuries, one false).

1. Bone fractures: a number of types depending on the nature of the break. Some of the most common are:

    A. Greenstick - bone is cracked and bent, but not completely broken off, usually found in children and may be compared to a break in a green twig when sharply bent.

    B. Closed (simple) - bone is broken, but not the skin.

    C. Open (Compound) - bone and skin are broken, bone protrudes through the skin.

    D. Comminuted - a bone is splintered at the site of the fracture, crushed.

    E. Impacted - ends of bone are telescoping.

    F. Multiple - bone is broken in more than one place.

    G. Oblique (Spiral) - break extends diagonally across the bone.

    H. Transverse - break extends across the bone, at right angles to its long axis.

Recognition of bone injury:

    A. Sound of a "click."

    B. Tenderness and swelling at point of injury.

    C. Crepitus or grating of the bone.

    D. Sudden stabbing pain on movement.

    E. Contraction of muscles in area.

    F. Deformity.

    G. Nausea (Shock Chapter XVI).

2. Nerve injury

    Recognition: Burning sensation - like being hit on the "crazy bone" - numb, pins, needles.

3. Muscle

4. Tendon

5. Ligament

Discomfort worse on movement, dull pain, perhaps over an elongated area, stiffening overnight; for ligament and tendon injuries, comparison of loose joint to opposite joint.

6. Joint

Effusion - fills up with fluid. If so, athlete may say his joint feels as though it is being gripped hard by a number of moving fingers.

7. Organ (Medical Emergency) See Chapter XII

(a) Contusion to kidney - possible blood in urine (hematuria), signs of shock, rigidity of back muscles. (b) Rupture of the spleen (requires surgical removal) - signs of shock (see Chapter XVI), abdominal rigidity, nausea; Kehr sign or pain radiating to left shoulder and 1/3 of the way down the left arm.

8. Compensation - in reality a false injury, often called a cause-and-effect injury. An athlete is injured in a specific area, and to relieve the pain in this area, he throws an undue strain on another area of the body. Before long, he feels as if he had been injured in the second area.

Classification of Injuries

1. Contusion (Above #1, 2, 3, 4, 5, 6, 7). A severe bruise with rupture of capillaries (Hematoma), nerves and involved tissue.

2. Strain (Above #2, 3, 4, 5, 6). Injury to muscular and tendinous tissue - capillaries and nerves.

3. Sprain (Above #4, 5, 6). Injury to ligamentous tissue - capillaries, nerves, bursae, capsule, etc.

Severity of Injury

1. Mild - fibers pulled apart, separated. Very little loss of function.

2. Moderate - fibers partially torn. Some loss of function.

3. Severe - fibers completely torn. Complete loss of function.

In all the above injuries, capillaries are torn. The blood will follow the capillary groove until the capillary is restored. An example of a torn capillary: if one slaps his arm hard, the arm will immediately turn red. This is blood from the broken capillaries.

Control of Hemorrhage

1. Reduce convalescent period greatly.
2. Reduce fibrous scarring of tissue.
    A. Ice
        1. Cold treatment should be used at least 45 minutes and continued for 24-48 hours if swelling persists.
        2. The advantages of cold are:
            a. It alleviates pain and makes the athlete feel better.
            b. Reducing the temperature of a cell reduces the metabolism of the cell and gives it a chance to come back again, like a runner who runs a mile, rests, and can then run again.
            c. Decreases capillary bleeding.
    B. Compression (to reduce flow of blood and lymph along with ice and elevation.)
        1. Place felt or sponge pad over area.
        2. Wrap with a wet elastic bandage, extend at least 6'' above and below the injury.
    C. Elevation
    D. Heat (Be careful, as heat will cause swelling).

General Treatment - Contusion, Strain, Sprain

Same as controlling hemorrhage - ice, compression, and elevation.

Recovery Time (Depending on severity of injury)

Most doctors list recovery time as follows:
1. Fractures
    A. Toes, fingers - three to four weeks.
    B. Elbow - splint for three weeks, and rehabilitation for three weeks.
    C. Major bone - minimum of six weeks.
2. Contusions, strains - two to twenty-one days
3. Sprains - seven to twenty-one days
4. Dislocations

    A. Major joint - 4 weeks
    B. Finger, Toe - after acute symptoms subside

General Rules - Treatment

1. Immediate
   A. A chemical cold agent used on the field.
   B. Ice, minimum 45 minutes.
   C. Compression, wet pressure bandage, if possible.
   D. Elevation, if possible.
   E. Ultrasound. (Use own judgment.)
   F. If no swelling:
      1. Light analgesic pack with support, or
      2. Support only.
   G. If swelling - support plus ice (no heat).
   H. **If in doubt refer to team physician.**
2. Second Day
   A. If swelling is severe:
      1. Pressure bandage, elevation and support.
      2. Cryotherapy (use of cold or ice).
   B. If no swelling or light swelling:
      1. Ice massage.
      2. Infra-red lamp - with or without wet towel.
      3. Whirlpool (follow whirlpool rules - Chapter II).
   C. Light massage above and below injury.
   D. Ultrasound.
   E. Contrast baths.
   F. Analgesic packs.
   G. Support.
3. Third Day
   If swelling, follow swelling rules; if not:
   A. Any of the above.
   B. Microtherm, only after 48 hours, especially in any injury (joints, etc.) where there is a chance of swelling.
   C. Steam packs.
   D. Paraffin bath.
   E. Traction.
   F. Massage.
   G. Contrast bath.
   H. Rehabilitative exercise, if possible.

    I.   Support, if necessary.

    J.   Ultrasound.

Heat may cause swelling - cold reduces swelling. Generally, one should use ice for acute injuries and heat for chronic injuries.

Alleviate fear, minimize injuries. If an individual is in shock, everything that is said will make a definite impression on him. If he is not in shock, do not say or do anything that will put him there.

As in all phases of athletics, the follow-through is important in the treatment of injuries, day or night if necessary.

1. Don't **Preach.**
2. Don't **Probe** too deeply.
3. Don't **Promise** too much.
4. Don't **Punish** with lectures.
5. Don't use **Platitudes** (trite utterances).

On the following four pages are diagrams showing the skeletal and muscular structure of the body. A knowledge of the names and locations of these parts is most essential and helpful in treating athletic injuries. Diagrams A, B, C, D.

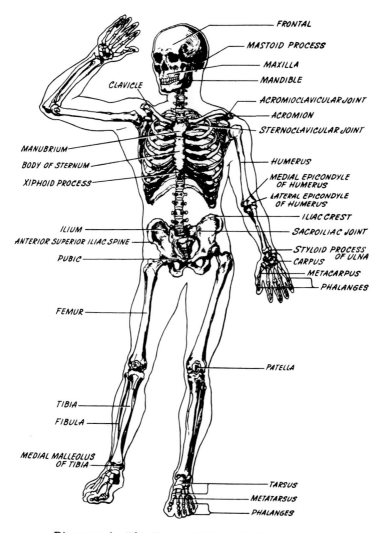

Diagram A. The Human Skeleton* (front view).

*Diagrams A and B supplied with compliments of Cramer Chemical Co., Gardner, Kansas.

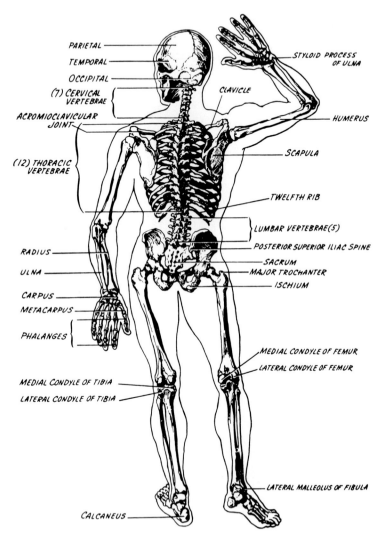

Diagram B. The Human Skeleton (rear view).

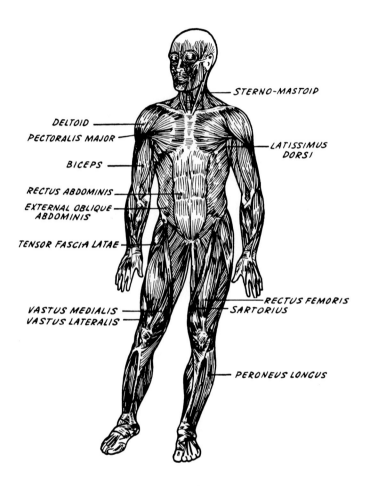

Diagram C. Muscles of the Body (front view).

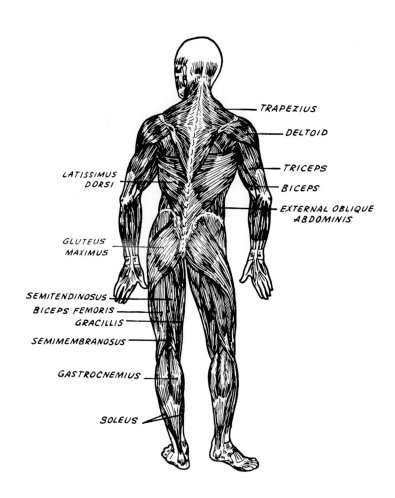

Diagram D. Muscles of the Body (rear view).

VIII

Taping and Bandaging,
Treating Skin Injuries,
Stopping Bleeding

Tearing Tape (Figure 1)

1. Have hands free of surface oil.
2. Be sure backing of the tape faces the trainer.
3. Firmly grasp the tape with thumbs held close to each other, and index fingers directly below the thumbs. Tape must be taut.

Figure 1. Tearing Tape.

4. Make a quick snap of the right wrist away from the body, and at the same time rotate the left wrist toward the body. Some will resist with the left wrist.
5. Remember that the secret is in breaking the first thread.
6. If not successful in tearing the tape in the first attempt, do not try again in the same place.

Rules For Taping

1. Prepare the skin - wash, shave, and apply tape adherent or tape directly to skin.
2. Use size of tape which fits the contour of the body.
3. Have the injured area in the position in which it is to remain.
4. Tape from the roll. Do not squeeze or ''bruise'' tape to insure uniform tension as the tape comes off the roll.
5. Apply smoothly, mold.
6. Strap firmly, avoid constriction and circular taping.
7. For support, tape directly to the skin.
8. Basketweave tape for additional strength at stress points.

9. Do not apply tape directly to nipples. Protect the nipple with a gauze pad.

10. Do not leave the tape on over two (2) days.

Care of Tape

Store tape in a cool dry place. If the tape gets too hot, store it in the freezer 2-3 days.

Rules For Applying Bandage

1. Be neat, clean, and thorough.
2. Use simplest application.
3. Have injured area in position it is to remain.
4. Anchor bandage so it will not slip. (Tape on start, or bandage on an angle).
5. Start at narrowest part of the limb and bandage toward heart.
6. Bandage firmly, but avoid constriction. Invert or evert (twist) the bandage.

Abrasions

Abrasions are rubbing off of the skin by mechanical means: floor burn, turf burn, strawberry, cinder burn.
Treatment:
1. Wash thoroughly with athletic liquid soap.
2. If debris (cinders) is in wound, use sterile forceps to remove.
3. Irrigate with hydrogen peroxide.
4. Apply zinc oxide or antibiotic ointment and cover with a telfa-pad which will not stick to the wound.
5. Do not permit a scab to form.

Laceration

Skin and tissue are torn with more or less jagged edges.
Treatment:
1. Use same treatment as for abrasions except wash the laceration lengthwise of the cut.
2. Refer to physician because suturing may be necessary.

Incised Wound

A straight-edged wound (''cut'').
Treatment:
1. Follow first three phases of treatment for abrasions.
2. If necessary, hold together with a butterfly closure (Figure 2) or make your own.
3. Refer to physician because suturing may be necessary.

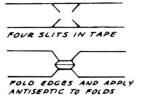

FOUR SLITS IN TAPE

Figure 2. Slitting tape.

FOLD EDGES AND APPLY
ANTISEPTIC TO FOLDS

Puncture Wound

Deep piercing wound (nail, spike).
1. Encourage bleeding.
2. Thoroughly wash and clean any foreign matter from wound.
3. Soak puncture area in a warm aseptic solution to keep it open.
4. Send to physician for probable tetanus shot. Use antibiotic ointment.

Blisters

Blisters are due to friction
Prevention:
1. Use tincture of benzoin (adherent) and powder.
2. Use skin lubricant.
3. Wear two pairs of socks.
4. Rub soap on the seams of the shoe or sprinkle soap flakes in socks.
5. Follow procedure for hot spots (Chapter IX).

Treatment:
A. If blister is filled with fluid
  1. Wash blister and surrounding area with alcohol.
  2. Open at back edge (1/2'' slit) with a sterile scalpel knife (Figure 3).

OPEN AT BACK EDGE

1/4" SLIT

Figure 3. Cutting a blister.

  3. Fill with antiseptic.
  4. Apply zinc oxide to a sterile gauze pad and cover.
  5. After blister has healed (2nd or 3rd day), trim away the loose skin. Bevel the edges.
  6. File or sandpaper the rough, loose edges of the skin and paint with tape adherent.
B. If blister is open - use same treatment as above.
C. If blister is infected
  1. Thoroughly clean blister and surrounding area (alcohol) and trim away all blistered skin and loose edges.
  2. Soak the foot in an alcohol and boric acid solution or in a boric acid solution.
  3. Apply an antibiotic and dress.
  4. See team physician.
D. Protection While Playing
  1. Cover blister with sterile dressing and cover with:
    a. Felt doughnut. Take a piece of 3/8'' felt and cut a hole in it, little larger than size of blister. Tape to hold in place.
    b. Spoon. Cut the handle off a spoon. Shape the spoon to fit the situation and tape over blister. Inner and side edges of spoon can be covered with thin layer of moleskin.

2. Cover blister with collodion.
3. If on back of heel, put felt heel pad in shoe to lift blister above shoe.

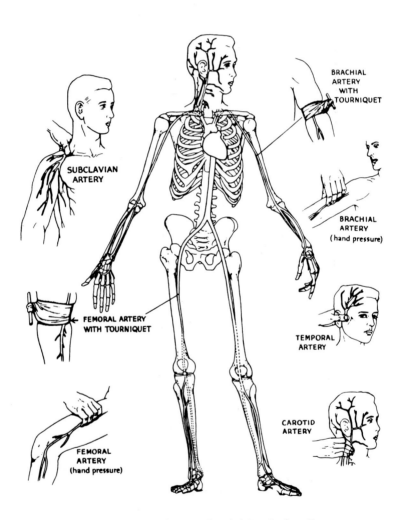

Figure 4. Courtesy of Cramer Chemical Co., Gardner, Kansas.

Control of Bleeding

Artery - characterized by a profuse flow of bright red blood, may be in spurts.

Vein - characterized by steady flow of dark red blood which may be of considerable volume but does not come in spurts.

Capillary - characterized by a steady ooze, is not serious and is easily controlled.

Treatment:

1. Hand pressure - use direct pressure on the wound by hand over a sterile gauze pad.

2. Pressure Bandage - firmly tie roller bandage or a half dozen gauze pads over the sterile gauze compress.

3. Pressure Points - In the more complicated and severe forms of bleeding (artery), apply pressure at a point where the artery is relatively near the surface and close to a bony structure. Enclosed chart illustrates the pressure points where arterial bleeding may be reached and checked (Figure 4).

4. Pneumatic Splints in place of tourniquet. Use pressure 20-30 mgs. of mercury to control venous oozing. For artery, use pressure compress — pneumatic splint — elevation.

5. Tourniquet - Last and least practical type of pressure. Physicians once taught that tourniquet should not be left on for over 15-20 minutes. However, some physicians now believe it should be left in place until loosened by a physician. (Figure 4).

6. Normal venous or capillary bleeding:
    a. Hydrogen peroxide or adrenalin chloride 1:1000.
    b. Doctor's recommendations: Gelfoam, surgicel.

7. Ice directly over wound (also helps prevent infection).

Closing Wounds

1. Bandage - paint surrounding area with adherent so dressing will hold longer. Use elastic tape as it will adhere better.

2. Butterfly (Figure 2).

3. Collodion.

4. Steri-strips.

5. Suturing by physician.

IX

Foot and Ankle Care

Introduction To Chapter IX Through Chapter XVI

Many excellent drugs, medications, ointments, etc. are now on the market. The following chapters will discuss what doctors are using along these lines at the present time. In years to come, as medical science discovers better medications, the trainer must keep abreast of these developments and work hand-in-hand with his team physician to insure athletes the very best and most modern treatment.

The following chapters will not go into detailed treatments of the various injuries as these were discussed in Chapter VII.

CHAPTER IX

Protection of the Feet

Condition the feet before the season starts by applying tincture of benzoin (adherent) twice per day. While the adherent is still "tacky" apply powder to the feet. Continue to use the adherent and powder after the season has started. You may also wish to wear two pairs of socks. If the inner seam of the shoe is bothersome, try rubbing soap on the seam.

Hot Spots

Recognition: A burning hot sensation on the bottom of the foot, but no fluid.

Treatment: Soak the foot in cold water for ten minutes or rub an ice massage on the hot spot. Rub a small amount of bland ointment in the hot spot before the next practice.

Bruise or Broken Toe

Recognition: Deformity, pain, tenderness, swelling.

Treatment: Immediately soak in cold water for a minimum of 45 minutes. Starting the second day, use whirlpool or soak in warm epsom salt solution.

Taping: Immobilize by taping the injured toe to the adjoining toe or toes, or place a collodion cast (gauze and collodion) around the toe.

Sprained Big Toe

Recognition and Treatment: Same as for bruised or broken toe.
Taping: Immobilize the joint. Secure a 3/8" felt pad to the foot.
(Figure 5). Tape the toe (Figure 6a-6b).
Protective Equipment: Same as for bruised or broken toe.

Figure 5. Taping sprained toe.

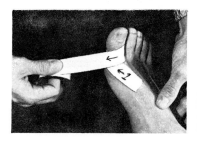

Figure 6 A. Taping of the big toe for Hyperextension. We tape toe downward. May use adhesive or elastic. Use as many strips as necessary.

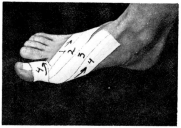

Figure 6 B. Taping for a hyperflexed toe. Tape upwards.

Blood Under Toe Nail

Treatment: Remove the blood by drilling through toe nail with the end of a knife or nail drill. Treat as an open wound.
Protection: Same as for a bruised or broken toe.

FOOT AND ANKLE CARE

Ingrown Toe Nail

Recognition: Inflamed and swollen area along the medial or lateral sides of the big toe nail. Toe nail has grown down into the skin.

Prevention: Wear proper fitting shoes and cut the nail straight across, not shorter than the flesh.

Treatment:
1. Soak in epsom salt until the nail is soft and pliable,
2. Soak a small piece of cotton in alcohol and force under the edges of the nail. This will lift and force the nail to grow properly.
3. Cover with collodion or a bandage.

Athlete's Foot

Recognition: A reddened, irritated area with or without blisters, caused by a fungus or plant parasite.

Prevention: Keep the area dry at all times; use foot powder; wear white cotton socks; do not wear rubber-soled shoes or rubber thongs.

Treatment: Dry thoroughly (don't rub harshly) between the toes at all times and use foot powder in shoes.
1. No Blister - most common. Spreads with perspiration; can be found anywhere on the body. Treat with Tinactin, Micatin.
2. Blister Type - Open blister and soak in potassium permanganate one hour two times a day. Use ultra-violet light or sun and follow with one of the above ointments or liquids.

Foot Odors and Perspiring Feet

Treatment:
1. Change the socks and shoes daily.
2. Do not wear rubber-soled shoes or nylon socks.
3. Wash feet thoroughly three times a day.
4. Soak feet in 1% formaldehyde in distilled water and follow with foot powder.
5. Dust feet with powdered alum or boric acid to absorb excessive perspiration. Sweating not induced by violent exercise may be caused by anxiety or other emotional stimuli.

Relax - may need guidance of a psychologically oriented physician.

Treatment: Lotion containing aluminum chloride (some people sensitive to it).

Hammer Toe

Recognition: Toes forced up in a claw-like position (Figure 7).
Prevention: Wear shoes that are of the proper length (long enough).
Treatment: Massage and force the joint down (Figure 7) or use felt pad (Figure 8a).

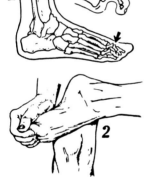

Figure 7. Hammer toes, showing affected skeletal structure.

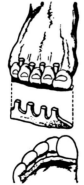

Figure 8a. Toe pad is cut from 1/4'' felt and used to hold or support the four lesser toes. Works well on a high arched foot, or a foot with prominent metatarsal area; or for hammer toes. Reduces friction on the ends of toes. Cut thinner under big toe to help hold pad in position.

63

Figure 8b. This is similar to preceding pad. In addition to the same results as preceding pad, the ring can be shaped for either second, third, or fourth toes *to act as a padding for a painful corn.* The hole must be cut large enough for the toe to fit through without tearing the felt.

Bunion

Recognition: Deformed big toe joint.

Prevention: Wear shoes of the proper length and width.

Treatment: Apply pad (Figure 9), with elastic tape. Do not tape too tightly as return to normal position must be gradual. Heat, whirlpool, and analgesic balm pack will remove soreness.

Figure 9. Application of Pad to Bunion.

Transverse Arch (Metatarsal) Injuries

Recognition: Severe pain just to the inside of the ball of the foot when the individual goes up on his toes (Figure 10).

Prevention: Wear proper footwear and run on a soft surface.

Treatment: (Figure 11). Attach pads with elastic tape.

Figure 10

Figure 10a. A cross-section of the metatarsal bones of a normal transverse arch. Normal pressure is on the first and fifth bones.

Figure 10b. A fallen transverse arch - pressure now on the second, third, and fourth metatarsal heads.

Figure 11

Figure 11A. This is the common metatarsal head pad. The important point is in the placing of the pad. The thickest part is back of the head and the feathered edge goes forward over the heads. The point of importance here is that the highest elevation is just behind the heads in order to pick them up. Use 1/4'' wool or cotton felt.

Figure 11b. This is a 1/4'' thick felt metatarsal pad with a cut-out for a definite painful area (x). The cut-out can be made to fit over any of the metatarsal heads desired. This takes the pressure off the painful spot and spreads it over painfree areas.

Figure 11

Figure 11c. This 1/4'' felt pad is used to divert pressure from a prominent big toe joint (1st metatarsal phalangeal joint), or a blistered or calloused area at this spot. Note that the pad must run down the shaft of the first metatarsal bone in order to give it support. Dotted line indicates approximate position of first metatarsal shaft.

Figure 11d. This is a cut-out pad for the commonly seen painful area under the 1st and 5th joints. Note the pad is NOT skived (beveled) on the forward end. This is to give support through this region and keep the weight off the 1st and 5th areas.

·Every pad used should aim toward correction of improper position of the foot and must insure comfort and permit relaxation. Testing and retesting for shape and thickness will pay dividends.

Stress Fracture (Fatigue or March Fracture) - Metatarsal

Cause: Long, continued or often repeated stress, like a fatigue fracture which sometimes occurs in metal.

Recognition: Symptoms of a fallen transverse arch plus extreme tenderness and a slight swelling on top of the foot, usually the third metatarsal.

Treatment: Place the foot in an orthopedic shoe or a plaster cast. Remove daily for 20 minutes of whirlpool treatment.

Taping: When doctor will permit, use an ''X'' strapping (Figure 12) and continue to encircle the foot snugly with adhesive tape down to base of the toes. Finish with a complete ankle strapping (Figure 17).

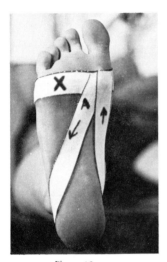

Figure 12 a

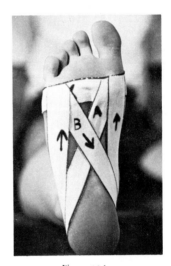

Figure 12 b

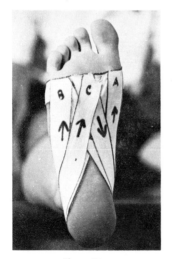

Figure 12 c

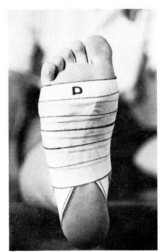

Figure 12 d

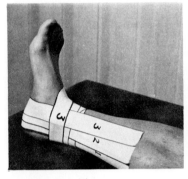

View 1

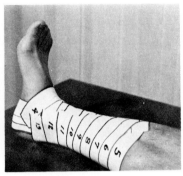

View 2

Figure 17

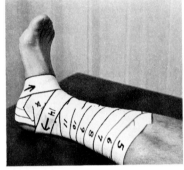

View 3

Longitudinal Arch

Recognition: Pain in the main arch of the foot.

Taping: (Figure 12).

Foot Rest (Addition to "X" Strapping): 1 inch strip of adhesive tape around side of foot from little toe to big toe. Fill in bottom (no tension) up to side strips from base of toes to heel. (Figure 12d).

Callus

Cause: Incorrectly fitting shoes, friction, pressure, weakening of transverse arch, etc.

Treatment: Remove the cause; file the callus down with a wood rasp, sandpaper, callus file, pedicor (do not use a razor blade because of the danger of cutting into live tissue). If the callus remains sore, soak in boric acid or sodium bicarbonate solution. To soften, place a salicylic acid plaster on the callus or put adhesive tape over it and leave for two to three days.

Corn (Hard)

Recognition: An overgrowth of skin (callus) which dips down and presses on nerves.

Treatment: Remove the pressure which caused the corn. File the corn as you would a callus (do not cut). To remove the remainder of the corn, use salicylic acid plaster corn pad. Paint with 10% salicylic acid in collodion. Ordinary tape left on corn for two to three days may cause it to soften and disappear. Use a pad for painful corn (Figure 8b).

Corn (Soft)

Recognition: A soft, white, flaky area usually with a small hole in the center, found between the toes, usually the last two toes.

Cause: Excessive sweating of feet; failure to clean and dry toes thoroughly; shoes that do not fit.

Treatment: Eliminate the cause; wash with alcohol; paint with 5% solution of silver nitrate; powder; keep toes apart and dry with felt or cotton.

Plantar Wart

Recognition: A very painful area on the sole of the foot (possibly on palm of hand) at level of head of metatarsals (Figure 13b). It looks like a small oval callus with a core. To aid in diagnosis, moisten wart with alcohol. If it is a plantar wart, there will usually be black spots under the callus.

Cause: Virus infection. It may be mildly contagious.

Treatment: Usually will have to be treated by a physician. Treatments often used are (1) salicylic acid tape for three or four days, rest three to four days and repeat. (2) Soak foot in hot water; cut a hole in a piece of moleskin; fill with 60% salicylic acid ointment, nitric acid or foot ointment; remove in three days. Coat surrounding normal skin with vaseline, etc. (3) Apply metatarsal pad to relieve pain (may result in a cure). (4) Use ultrasound.

Doctor's Recommendation: Electric needle.

Stone Bruise

Cause: A severe bruise on bottom of heel affecting soft tissue and possibly bone.

Treatment: Apply ice immediately. Second day use whirlpool and analgesic balm packs.

Taping: (Figure 13a and 13b).

Special Protective Equipment: Make a heel cup out of fiber glass or out of a tablespoon (cut handle off spoon; flatten front and sides slightly, back part will fit contour of heel; tape to heel, fine for protecting bruises anywhere on foot or ankle). Commercial heel cups may also be purchased.

Doctor's Recommendation: Steroid, enzyme, local anesthetic, anti-inflammatory agents.

PROTECTION FOR
"STONE BRUISE"

STONE
BRUISE
PAD

PLANTAR
WART

– A –   – B –

Figure 13a. Basketweave tape (1/2'' or 1'') with extreme force. Figure 8 taping (1-1/2'') then applied over basketweave to secure loose ends.

Figure 13b. Cut a piece of sponge rubber (Figure 6) or felt (1/4'') to fit the heel - cut a hole in the rubber slightly larger than the tender area. Secure pad to heel with adhesive tape.

Blood Blister - Edge of Heel

Recognition: A hard, crusted, dark callused area along the edge of the heel.

Cause: Lateral sliding of foot in the shoe, friction, pinching.

Treatment: File the area as explained under treatment of calluses; use whirlpool, analgesic balm packs.

Taping: Same as for stone bruise (Figure 13a and 13b).

Heel Spur - Callus

Recognition: Pain, tenderness, swelling, callus-like enlargement on heel, just below where top of low-cut shoes stop.

Cause: Improper shoes; pressure, bruise, friction, injury to calcaneus (heel bone).

Treatment: Whirlpool, analgesic balm packs.

Taping Methods: Cut a piece of felt in the shape of a doughnut and tape over the area. This will relieve pressure and possibly the tenderness will disappear. (2) Place a heel pad in the shoe. (3) Use tablespoon as explained under stone bruise.

Doctor's Recommendation: Surgery.

Tendinitis

Recognition: An irritation and inflammation of any tendon sheath (top of foot, achilles tendon, wrist, etc.). Feeling and sometimes sound like crinkly wax paper as tendon moves in swollen sheath. Pain, crepitation.

Cause: Bruise, blow, pressure, poor condition, change from one sport to another.

Treatment: Heat and rest. Alternate whirlpool (100° - 102°) and Microtherm daily, analgesic balm packs in between, perhaps splint for complete rest (remove splint for heat).

Taping: Apply a snug bandage with a sponge rubber heel pad.

Doctor's Recommendations: Skeletal muscle relaxant, steroid, enzyme, local anesthetic, anti-inflammatory agents.

Achilles Tendon Strain

Recognition: Pain along the tendon when the toe is flexed,

Figure 14. Taping to shorten the tendon. View is of the heel of the foot.

occasionally where toe is extended. Also, with the athlete on his stomach, foot relaxed at a right angle, the trainer may squeeze his calf. If the tendon is ruptured, the foot will not flex, or sometimes it may flex inward.

Cause: Sudden strain or blow.

Treatment: Ice immediately followed by treatment rules.

Taping: Tape to shorten the tendon. Extend the toe and tape as illustrated in Figure 14. Start first strip of tape (1 1/2'') behind ball of foot and extend up to calf. Begin second and third strips on top of instep, down under heel and cross on Achilles tendon, leaving ankle bone free. Repeat strips 1-2-3 and anchor below calf, above ankle bones and over arch. Use a sponge rubber heel pad in practice and street shoe.

If injury pains when the toe is extended, just reverse the above taping method. Flex the toe, start first strip behind toes on top of foot and extend up the shin, second and third strips in front of the leg.

Doctor's Recommendations: Same as for Tendonitis.

Ankle Sprain

Mechanism of Injury: The ankle bone does not turn, twist, or rotate when injury occurs. The heel bone (Calcaneum) is turned under, causing ligaments to separate. The heel bone is the key to stability (Calcaneum-Talus).

A fairly conservative estimate is that eighty-five per cent of ankle injuries are inversion injuries. (Figure 15b). These injuries may be classified for diagnosis and treatment as follows:

    A. Type of Injury

        1. Inversion (inversion, internal rotation, plantar flexion).

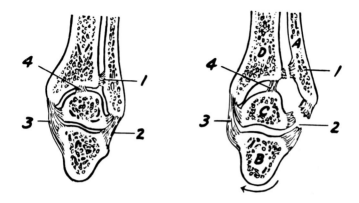

Figure 15a. View of a normal right ankle (from rear) showing ligaments that may be sprained. (1) Anterior Tibiofibular Ligament. (2) Lateral Collateral Ligament. (Calcaneofibular). (3) Medial Collateral (Deltoid) Ligament. (4) Anterior Astragalus - Tibial Ligament.

Figure 15b. Diagrammatic figure of most commonly sprained ligaments. (A) Fibula. (B) Calcaneum. (C) Astrangalus or Talus. (D) Tibia.

2. Eversion (eversion, external rotation, dorsal flexion).
B. Diagnosis
  History - Time of injury; manner of injury, direction of force degree of disability, time of onset, pain, swelling, deformity.
C. Examination
  1. Observation - Deformity, discoloration, welling.
  2. Palpation - Tension of skin, crepitation, range of motion, abnormal motion.
  3. X-ray.
D. Degree of Injury (Refer to Chapter VII - **Severity of Injury**)
  1. Mild - Fibers pulled apart, separated, very little loss of function.
  2. Moderate - Fibers partially torn, some loss of function.
  3. Severe - Fibers completely torn, complete loss of function.
E. Mild Sprain
  1. Diagnosis - local swelling, tenderness, pain, and mild disability, X-ray negative.

73

2. Treatment - pressure, ice, local injection, heat, strapping, and continued activity.

F. Moderate Sprain
   1. Diagnosis - more pain, swelling disability, and pain on reproducing stress and on normal motion, X-ray negative.
   2. Treatment - (designed to prevent further injury). Pressure and ice, (30 minutes to overnight), injection, heat (no sooner than ten hours), splints, walking cast, strapping.

G. Severe Sprain
   1. Diagnosis - Positive: severe early swelling, pain, and disability. Pain on normal motion. Abnormal motion possible. Possible X-ray findings.
   2. Treatment
      a. Non-surgical: same as for moderate sprain.
      b. Surgical: complete repair, splint ten days, walking cast ten days, strap.

To check for bone involvement, compress the tibia and fibula above the malleoli simultaneously. Pain above the malleoli indicates a potential fracture; pain below the malleoli indicates a potential sprain.

Prevention: An ounce of prevention is worth a pound of cure. For this reason trainers often require all athletes (football and basketball) to wear either tape or the Louisiana Lock ankle wrap (Figure 16). By wearing this ankle wrap an athlete who may be injured will suffer an injury one degree less than it would have been had he not had the wrap on. Some schools have had fine success by requiring their athletes to wear ankle wraps 2 1/4'' wide and 96'' in length. They can be purchased in 72 yard rolls and cut to desired lengths.

A good device is a basketweave with a heel-lift using 1 1/2'' tape. All taping is done directly to the skin (taping rules, Chapter VIII).

The trainer taping for preventive purposes should have the athlete hold his foot so it is perpendicular to the floor. If he is trying to protect a lateral sprain, he instructs the athlete to hold his foot perpendicular with a slight outward rotation (shorten ligaments on lateral side of ankle). Reverse procedure used if injury is to inside of ankle. The following views refer to the illustration in Figure 17.

View 1. Start the first perpendicular strip of tape a minimum of 4'' above the ankle bone on the inside rear of the leg, carry it down under the heel and up the outside of the leg to just below the calf

LOUISIANA ANKLE WRAP*

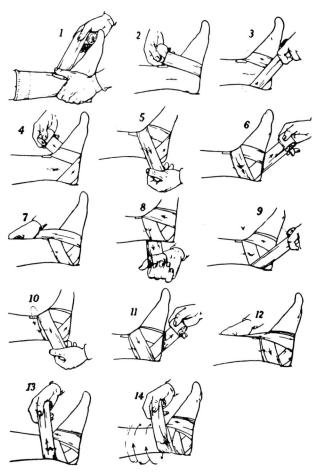

Figure 16: "Louisiana Ankle Wrap." Apply over a sweat sock. The sock will act as a cushion against cutting into the skin.

The wrap is approximately 96 inches long. No. 1 starts on top, but here again there is a difference of opinion. Some start around the foot, some around the leg. At Oklahoma, we start on the foot.

Follow the diagram as illustrated from figures No. 1 to and including No. 14.

In No. 13, the "heel-lock" is completed and the balance of the wrap is carried around the leg (No. 14) to afford a cushion against bruising blows.

In No. 14 finish wrap above ankle. Use 1-1/2" adhesive and anchor entire ankle with same procedure as above.

(View 1). Start the first circular strip just above the ankle bone and completely encircle the leg.

View 1. Let the second perpendicular strip overlap the first, from a fanning top to more of an overlap over the joint. Have second circular strip overlap circular strip number one.

View 1. For third perpendicular and circular strips follow same lines (overlapping) for the second trips.

View 2. Anchor fourth strip at top of arch.

View 2. Overlap circular strips 5-13 as they work down the leg from circular strip number 5. (Start of heel lock).

View 3. Strip 14 is start of double heel lock (both sides of ankle), complete ankle-taping. Be sure not to leave any open spaces along the Achilles tendon to cause a pinching or blistering. Heel lock is same procedure as in ankle wrap (Figure 16).

Special Protective Equipment

For an extremely weak ankle, incorporate a felt horse shoe on the injured side of the ankle. This will permit freedom of flexion and extension, but will prevent inversion and eversion.

To determine whether an ankle is strong enough to practice, have the athlete run in circles to right and left. If there is no limp, the athlete should be able to practice.

Doctor's Recommendation: Enzyme, steroids, anti-inflammatory agents.

Rehabilitative Exercises: See Chapter XV for specific exercises for ankle arch and lower leg.

X

Lower Leg, Knee, and Thigh Conditions and Injuries

Shin Splints

Recognition: Pain on either side of lower 1/3 of shin bone, often a roughened area (similar to small grains of sand) along the bone as finger runs gently up and down the bone.

Cause: Dealing with shin splints means dealing with a multitude of different causes. All of the causes could be true. Some of the beliefs are that shin splints are due to a dropping of the arch which sets up a reaction in the five tendons of the lower leg; irritation of interosseus membrane (between tibia and fibula); an inflammation (many minute ruptures of muscle) of the tibial periosteum; muscle spasm caused by swelling of anterior tibial muscle; a strain of soleus or tibialis posterior muscle; periostitis at attachment of tibialis muscle to tibial crest. Other possible causes are listed under prevention.

Prevention: The athlete himself should be responsible for most preventive work and should observe certain steps: (1) Start early (arches strapped) and work gradually into shape. (2) Run low on the foot; do not get up on the toes. (3) Run in tennis shoes (no spikes). (4) Beware of hard surfaces; run on grass. (5) Reverse directions in running, not always to the left. (6) Run backwards. (7) Rock from heel to toe. (8) On back, raise right leg perpendicularly and touch opposite left hip with head and shoulders flat. Repeat with left leg. (9) On back, grasp knees, and pull up to chin. Rock back and forth. Low back strain possible cause. (10) Sitting, extend foot with toes curled and grasp hand of trainer, who forces foot back against resistance. Repeat, starting with foot flexed. (11) Run and walk pigeon toed.

Treatment: There is nothing better than complete rest and heat around the clock (whirlpool 100-104 degrees, Hydrocollator, analgesic balm packs on shin and low back). Wear a sponge heel pad at all times. Some prefer a pad right up to base of big toe. Some trainers will not tape an athlete's shin unless he can get twenty minutes of heat before practice. Some require twenty minutes of ice massage after practice.

Taping: There are almost as many methods as trainers. In a popular method, the trainer applies an "x" longitudinal arch strapping (Figure 12).

Other methods of support are:

1. Apply a double weave, same as Figure 18 only alternate the starting point from the outside to the inside, etc.

2. Place a piece of sponge rubber 1" wide along the shin and

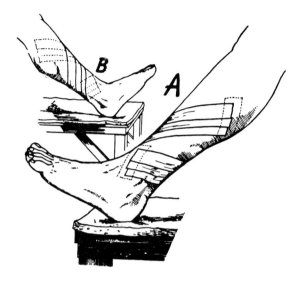

Figure 18. *Shin Splint.* Start on the outside of the leg just above the ankle with 1-1/2''
adhesive tape. Spiral behind the leg, and as you come to the shin area use your free
hand to push the excess skin and tissue in towards the shin bone. Then as tape comes
across the irritated shin it will hold the above tissue, protecting it from further
irritation. Anchor tape at top and bottom as indicated by dotted lines. Figure B indicates how it will look from the opposite side. If desired, entire area can then be
wrapped with an elastic wrap. If irritation is on the outside of the shin, reverse the
above procedure. If both sides of the shin are injured, apply a double weave - same as
above, only alternate the starting point from outside to inside, etc.

hold snugly with adhesive tape or an elastic wrap.

3. Tape a felt pad under arch and big toe.

4. Extend the ankle and apply three 1 1/2'' strips of tape around
the ball of the foot, then flex the ankle tightly and apply two strips
around the shin 3'' above the ankle bone.

5. Use elastic stockings.

6. Start 1 1/2'' tape at base of fifth metatarsal (prominent bone
on outside of foot). Bring under foot and up inside of leg and cross
over and finish under head of fibula (outside of leg). Repeat on other
side if necessary. Finish with rest of strapping.

Doctor's Recommendation: Enzyme, Vitamin B_{12}.

Varicose Vein

A problem for the team physician. However, a boy can be given relief if he will wear an elastic stocking.

Muscle Cramps - Heat Cramps

Recognition: A severe contraction of any muscle in the body.

Causes: Fatigue; lack of sodium and potassium; sudden exposure to cold; muscle made to do things to which it is unaccustomed; improper warm-up; lack of stretching exercises.

Prevention: Graduated stretching exercises throughout the preseason and season, sodium and potassium, and cool electrolyte solution.

Treatment: Relieving muscle cramps (1) Lengthen the muscle; stretch it. (2) Restore the circulation; use heat and vigorous massage. (3) Use salt, potassium, calcium, and a cool electrolyte solution.

Doctor's Recommendation: Replace fluids and electrolytes.

Why take sodium tablets? The drinking of large quantities of water without a proportionate intake of sodium is harmful in that it leads to more profuse sweating and a greater loss of sodium from the body. Sodium ingestion is essential for proper tissue metabolism for the body tissues cannot store sodium. It must be replaced daily.

Heat Exhaustion

Quite Common - not really serious.

Cause - Hot, humid weather; working in tight heavy clothing; heavy exercise; poor physical condition; overwork; lack of salt and water.

Recognition -

Sweating profusely which may turn into a cold, clammy sweat. Temperature normal or slightly elevated.

Faint feeling, pale face.

Weak rapid pulse.

Shallow breathing.

Nausea, headache.

Exhaustion, collapse.

Loss of consciousness.

Treatment -

Treat for shock

Elevate legs above head.

Place in well-ventilated room.

Remove clothing.

Use electric fan on patient to cool.

Give saline or quick-acting salt.

Heat Stroke (Sunstroke)

Less common - quite serious.

Cause - Hot humid weather; physical exertion; lack of salt and water; direct sun rays; use of alcohol.

Recognition -

* * * No sweating
* * * Hot dry skin

Temperature high - 106 to 112.

Chest pains.

Skin flushed, may turn grey (serious).

Strong, rapid pulse.

Labored breathing.

Nausea, headache.

Exhaustion, collapse, convulsions.

Loss of consciousness.

Contraction, then dilation, of pupils.

Treatment -

Call or take to doctor (if you take to doctor wrap in wet sheets and keep cold on way to hospital).

Cool the individual the best way you can. Put in bathtub full of ice until temperature is at least 100, or wrap in wet sheets, fan, or place in chair in a cold shower.

Keep in low semi-reclining position (may be too hard on heart to recline completely).

Give saline or quick-acting salt tablets.

Bandage legs from ankles to thigh.

Put in lukewarm shower, clothes and all.

Sponge with ice packs, especially forehead, neck and wrist.

Use ammonia capsule.

Massage extremities lightly.

Osgood-Schlatter Fracture

Recognition: It is actually not a fracture and it is not a knee injury. It is a forcible separation of the tibial tubercle, the projection of the anterior head of the tibia. In youth, the connection between the main bone and the head of the bone is soft. (It hardens with age). When the athlete sits on a table and bends his knee, the bone pushes out into the flesh (Figure 19). It goes back in place when the leg is straight.

Cause: An injury of early teen-aged youths, due to a blow, jumping.

Treatment: Relieve the pain and tenderness. Use whirlpool, microtherm, hydrocollator, ultrasound with analgesic balm packs in between.

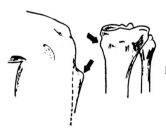

Figure 19. Osgood-Schlatter knee fracture.

Taping: With the athlete standing, tape snugly immediately below the tibial projection (may use a felt pressure pad below injury). Finish by completely encircling that area of the leg with elastic adhesive tape.

Protective Equipment: Have athlete wear at least a sponge rubber knee pad. It may be necessary to improvise a doughnut pad out of plastic or make a pad out of fiber glass to keep the pressure off the injured area.

Doctor's Recommendation: If the injury is discovered early enough a splint can be placed on the back of the leg. This will prevent the knee from bending long enough to permit the disease to heal (3-5 weeks). Another possibility is surgery.

Knee Injuries

In Figure 20 the two main bones of the knee (femur and tibia) have been separated to show the articular surfaces between the bones with the semilunar cartilages C and D. A and B are the anterior and posterior cruciate ligaments. They are called cruciate because they cross each other like the lines of a letter X. E is the patellar ligament with the infra-patellar bursa (a sack containing fluid found or formed over an exposed and prominent part, or where a tendon plays over a bone - approximately 13 in and around the joint). The cruciates are two of the ten ligaments which hold the joint in position.

Figure 21 shows what may happen when an athlete is clipped from the outside of the knee as shown by the single arrow. The dotted line indicates normal relationship while the solid line illustrates the angle produced by the blow. The figure shows the increase of pressure on the lateral cartilage at A and the release of pressure at B - with the double arrow showing over-extension of the medial collateral

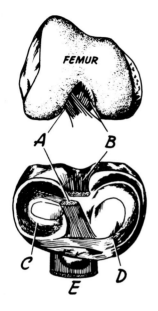

Figure 20. View of normal knee.

ligament. The patella (knee cap) has been turned down on its ligament revealing the articular surface of the knee cap and the femur. The medial collateral ligament C is long and fan-shaped. It is part of the joint capsule and its deep layer is attached to the medial cartilage. The lateral collateral ligament D is long and cord-like; it is not a part of the capsule and the lateral cartilage is not attached to it.

A knee demands **early**, careful examination. The trainer should note especially:

(1) Severity of injury, (2) degree of disability, (3) abnormal motion, (4) location of tenderness, (5) amount and rapidity of swelling, (6) restriction of pain on normal motion, (7) locking.

The knee injury may be mild, moderate or severe. For example:

A. Mild - some fibers of ligament damaged, no loss of strength of ligament.

B. Moderate - Definite tear in ligament, loss of strength.

C. Severe - Complete tear of ligaments and complete loss of integrity.

Generally, with a mild knee injury there will be no practice missed, but treatment should be administered. With a moderate knee

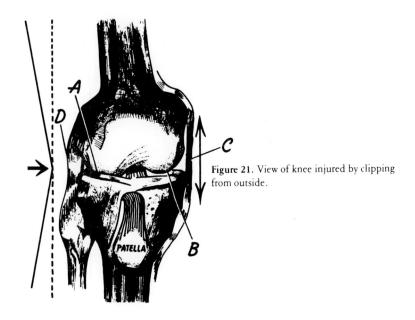

Figure 21. View of knee injured by clipping from outside.

sprain the athlete may miss from one to seven days practice and treatment should be administered. In the event of a severe knee injury the athlete will be out for a prolonged period of time and will require a physician's care.

The symptoms for a mild knee sprain are classified into two groups, positive and negative.

A. Positive - (1) tender at site of tear, (2) pain on abnormal stress, (3) local swelling, (4) pain on forced motion.

B. Negative - (1) no instability, (2) no blood in joint, (3) no effusion, (4) no locking, (5) no pain on normal motion.

Treatment for the mild knee sprain is: (1) rest, (2) cold, then heat, (3) protection, (4) injection (local, enzyme, steroid, procaine, etc.), (5) early active motion, (6) no immobilization, (7) anti-inflammatory agents.

The common symptoms for the moderate knee sprain are:

A. Positive - (1) pain in knee, (2) local tenderness, (3) disability, (4) swelling, (5) fluid in joint, (6) pain on stress, (7) locking.

B. Negative - no abnormal mobility.

The treatment for the moderate knee sprain is: (1) pressure, (2) cold, then heat, (3) rest, (4) aspiration of joint, (5) protection (splint,

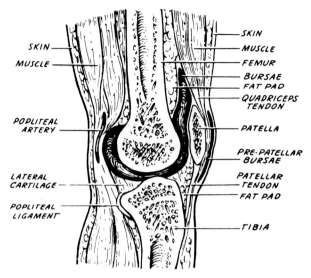

Figure 22. Knee Joint - Longitudinal Cross section, Lateral View.

cast, tape cast), (6) rehabilitation (very important).

The symptoms for a severe knee sprain are: (1) immediate disability, (2) inability to use knee, (3) severe pain, (4) abnormal motion, (5) blood in joint, (6) blood infiltration, (7) marked swelling, (8) locking, (9) positive X-ray.

The non-surgical treatment for the severe knee sprain is the same as for the moderate sprain. The surgical treatment for the severe knee sprain is: (1) prompt decision, (2) early repair, (3) complete repair of all torn ligaments, (4) repair, not reconstruction.

Knee Injuries

Prevention: Strengthen the quadriceps and hamstrings in both legs and maintain a good balance between the hamstrings and quads in each leg.

Examination: Be systematic, and thorough; watch the eyes because they will indicate pain; check the patella; compare the knees (contour, discoloration, swelling - hot indicates infection); check joint-line (cartilage groove) and ligaments from origin to insertion (if torn,

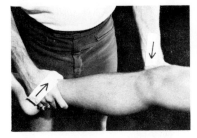

Figure 23 a . Medial collateral ligament test. Grasp leg with both hands as pictured. Attempt to move lower leg toward you, holding knee steady. Do not use force. Look for excessive tenderness and joint movement.

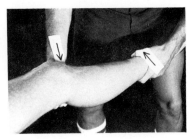

Figure 23 b . Lateral collateral ligament test. As pictured, attempt to move the lower leg away from you, holding the knee steady.

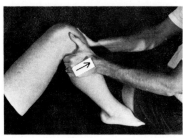

Figure 23 c . Cruciate ligament test. Check forward and backward motion in the joint (drawer test). This test may also be accomplished by letting the knee drop over the end of the table (as in figure 29) and then checking the forward and backward motion. There is normally a 1/4'' movement.

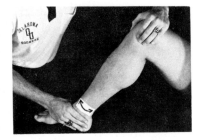

Figure 23 d Cartilage test. Place thumb against lower edge of the patella and move gently along the joint line as you lightly rotate, flex and extend the leg. An over all test — ligaments and cartilage. Use different degrees of pressure with right hand while moving lower leg with left hand. Check for grating and looseness.

there will be a roughness like particles of sand or rice); check size of quadriceps for atrophy (indication of an old injury).

Modify a knee test to fit the conditions, including swelling, tenderness, and stiffness. Carry out the test with the knee straight and also with a slight bend in the knee with the muscles relaxed and with the muscles flexed. **The important test is the test with the knee**

straight. Start all tests on the good knee. This will give the patient confidence that you are not going to hurt him and you can also use it for comparison. The cartilage and joint-line are one and the same thing. While checking a knee, keep one hand on or as close as possible to this joint line all the time. You may pick up a crackling, clicking sensation which will indicate a cartilage injury or a joint mouse and you will also be able to feel joint movement.

Cartilage Tests: (1) Any of the ligament tests, (2) Figure 23D, (3) Diagnosis of torn medial cartilage is often clinched by the following maneuver: Have patient in sitting position, ask him to put a little weight on the heel of the involved side, then slowly rotate his foot outward. Pain along the medial joint line is indicative of a torn medial cartilage. When the foot is rotated inward, pain on lateral joint indicates a possible injured lateral cartilage, (4) Locking: (a) torn cartilage, (b) joint mouse - a small section of bone, cartilage or ex-soft tissue broken off from its attachment. This mouse floats all around the knee and may cause an irritation or locking of the joint.

Reduction of Displaced Cartilage: Medial cartilage is injured six to eight times more frequently than the lateral cartilage. Often it is possible to slip a cartilage back into its groove. However, there are occasions when a knee becomes locked and it is impossible to unlock it manually. If this should occur, the knee will require surgery.

1. Have patient sitting on table, with leg over side of table, relax and swing the leg forward and backward and at the same time add internal and external rotation, alternately. This enlarges the joint and tends to loosen the cartilage.

2. Slowly flex and extend the knee with light outward and inward pressure.

3. Place arm behind the knee joint and slowly flex the knee (this will open up the joint) and then exert light outward and inward pressure.

4. Place patient on his back, grasp patient's ankle and exert a light pull (traction) on the leg while lightly rotating the knee in and out.

5. Keep patient on his back, flex knee to chest. If a medial cartilage, place one hand on the arch of the foot and gently pull the leg out laterally, and at the same time exert inward pressure with the other hand (fingers on cartilage line if possible). Shake the knee. With leg in this position (external rotation) bring it out into full extension.

6. Same as Number 5. Only rotate the knee in outward and

87

inward circles while flexed on the chest (fingers on joint-line as this may enable you to push the cartilage back in). Finish by bringing knee to extension as in Number 5.

Taping Method

Use a double weave (inside and outside of joint) with 3'' elastic adhesive tape. If additional support is necessary:

1. Incorporate regular adhesive with the elastic tape.

2. Include a felt pressure pad on the weak side of the knee put on after strip #6 (Figure 24e).

3. Incorporate the taping for an over-extended knee (Figure 24b) along with the regular knee-taping method.

Determine the amount of flexion and extension permitted by the angle of the knee joint at the start of the taping (the straighter the knee, the less movement), and by the tension on the elastic tape (for a tight taping, take all the elastic stretch out of the tape). The tape should come quite close to the patella, but should not touch it any time. If taping with regular and adhesive tape, fold the edges over as they cross the knee joint to prevent the tape from tearing.

24A - Begin with a 4'' x 4'' gauze pad directly behind knee and anchor with 3'' elastic tape (strip #1).

24B - (Strap for hyperextension and cruciate ligaments). Perform above (24A) and continue with strips numbers '4' vertically from lower 1/3 of hamstrings to upper 1/3 of calf. Proceed with 24C, 24D, 24E, and 24F.

24C - Use strips 5-9 to anchor basketweave strips 2 and 3. (Do not go all the way around leg).

24D - Start strip #1 on the lateral side of the leg, behind the calf and angle up above the patella (as close as possible to the patella) and end on the inside of the thigh. Start strip #2 on the outside of the thigh, angle below the patella (as close as possible) and end behind the calf on or near the start of strip #1. Begin strip #3 behind the calf on the outside of the leg and angle up under the patella (as close as possible) and end on the inside of the thigh. Start strip #4 on the outside of the thigh, angle down above the patella (as close as possible) and end behind the calf of the leg.

24E - Basketweave strips 5-6-7-8 over and have same angles as strips 1-2-3-4 with considerable overlap of each strip. Have strips 1 & 5 follow the same contour and angle as do strips 2&6, 3&7, and 4&8.

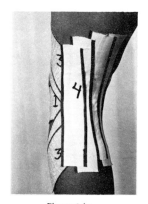

Figure 24 a

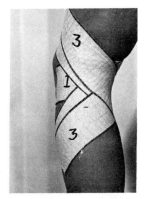

Figure 24 b

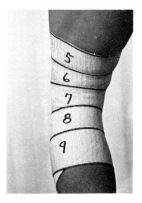

Figure 24 c

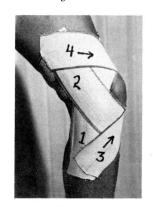

Figure 24 d

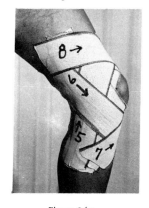

Figure 24 e

Figure 24 f

24F - Anchor at thigh with 3'' elastic (strips #9). Anchor strip #10 at calf. (Be careful not to get this strip too tight).

Doctor's Recommendation: Many physicians prefer to remove a torn cartilage as it is composed of fibro-cartilage which does not repair itself, and therefore recurrence is certain and eventual removal will be necessary. Aspirate (drain) any fluid that may be present. Drugs used for various types of knee injuries: steroids, enzymes.

Hyperextension Test

Keep knee straight. Support ankles with left hand and with very gentle force, press down on knee cap. Pain in back of knee will indicate over-extension.

Cruciate Ligaments or Hyperextension (Figure 23c)

Taping Method (Figure 24 a-f)

Fluid on Knee

A good way of detecting this is by the "ratellar click." With the knee straight, place one hand palm down over the lower end of the quadriceps (approximately one inch above the patella) with light pressure toward the toes. With index finger of other hand, gently press the patella down, release it and press down again. If fluid is present, there will be a click similar to two ice cubes striking together in a glass of water.

Treatment: In treatment of fluid on the knee, follow the rules in Chapter VII with special emphasis on pressure and ice. Follow above treatment with a pressure bandage over sponge rubber compress.

Doctor's Recommendation: Aspirate (removal of fluid). This should be done as soon as possible, one way or another. Steroids, enzymes.

Knee Braces

Many trainers prefer to tape knees; however, there are commercial braces that are adequate.

Tests to Determine if Knee is Strong Enough to Practice

1. The motor for the knee is the quadriceps (thigh) muscle. It runs the knee joint. If it is well developed, the knee will go. If not, it will collapse. The circumference of the thigh above the injured knee should be equal to or greater than the circumference of the opposite thigh. This can be determined by: (a) measuring eight inches up the thigh from the top of the knee cap and then measuring the circumference (some feel this is not an accurate way of testing as it is possible to elevate the patella from 1/2 to 3/4 of an inch); (b) measure from the anterior superior end of the spine of the pelvis 10-15 inches down the thigh and then measure the circumference; (c) measure the circumference of the thigh, 4, 6, and 8 inches above the top of the knee cap.
2. Running tests as described under ankles (Chapter XV).

Charley Horse

A charley horse or muscle contusion is a bruise type of injury. It is caused by a blow from the outside which damages the soft tissues, blood vessels, and nerves and may cause the muscle to go into spasm. It differs completely from a strain or pull.

Recognition: Tenderness, inability to run fast, possibility of a lump or muscular spasm. It is possible for a deep charley horse to damage the periosteum of the bone. If so, in the process of repair there may be a calcification in the muscle or on the bone. This condition, called myositis ossificans, usually does not show on an X-ray for three to four weeks. This is a problem for the team physician (see Chapter XIV) (Upper Arm Bruise).

Prevention: (1) Wear thigh pads slightly to the outside of the legs. (2) Wear over-sized thigh pads.

Treatment: If possible, have the player immediately kneel down and stretch the muscle (catcher's position) or fold leg under his body and sit on it. This prevents muscle contraction and hemorrhage. Follow with pressure bandage, ice, (with knee in full flexion), and general treatment rules. The player should start to jog as soon as possible as jogging will aid in recovering unless he has a **very** severe injury.

Figure 25. Taping Charley horse.

Taping Method (Figure 25): Have patient stand, heel elevated 1 1/2''. Use 1 1/2'' tape and start the semi-circular strapping well below and work upward (overlapping each strip) over and above the injury. Then apply diagonal (X) strips from the lower corners to the upper corners. Finish by encircling the leg with 3'' elastic tape or an elastic thigh cap.

Doctor's Recommendation: Enzymes, skeletal muscle relaxants, steroids, anti-inflammatory agents.

Protective Equipment: Build up the edges of the thigh pad to leave an air space between the leg and thigh pad where the injury is located.

Exercises: Under thigh in Chapter XV.

Hamstring Strain

This condition may occur in the belly or tendon of the muscle. Usually there is no advance warning and injuries have a tendency to recur as fibrous scar tissue replaces the muscle tissue.

Recognition: Patient will give a history of a sharp, snapping sensation and will be able to point out the exact spot of the pain. Often the athlete will fall or it will be necessary for him to stop his activity immediately. About the third day the leg will discolor below site of the injury. If the injury is a mild strain, the muscle will tighten and the athlete will have to slow up.

Causes:

1. Many so-called strains, perhaps mental, used as a crutch by some athletes.

2. A careless care-free warm-up (One should warm-up again if there is more than one half-hour between events).

3. Poor condition.
4. A lack of stretching exercises.
5. Fatigue cramps. Result in loss of oxygenation.
6. Lack of sodium.
7. A sudden change in temperature.
8. A sudden change of directions, loss of stride.

Treatment: General treatment rules plus analgesic balm pack on low back.

Functional Tests: (1) Turn athlete on his back, place one hand on the boy's knee to keep it straight and with the other hand holding the ankle attempt to raise the leg to a right angle. Determine the severity of the injury by the height the leg can be raised and compare with good leg. (2) Have athlete squat down with arms between legs and finger tips on the floor and raise the buttocks up so the legs are straight.

Taping Methods: Always wear a sponge heel pad on the leg affected. There are many trainers who do not believe in taping a hamstring strain. Many, however, use the following methods:

1. If the strain is in the belly of the muscle, use the same taping method as explained under charley horse (Figure 25) with one exception: place a piece of felt 5 by 8 by 1/2 inch right over the injured area before taping. This acts as a pressure pad. Also, apply the encircling strips with an uplifting stress. Lift the belly of the muscle and shorten the pull and finish by encircling the leg with 3'' elastic adhesive or an elastic thigh cap.

2. If a light strain is in the belly of the muscle, encircle the leg with a 2'' strip of adhesive 2 inches above the knee and then place another strip around the leg just under the buttocks.

Test to Determine if Athlete is Ready to Participate - When he can do the functional tests, he is ready.

Doctor's Recommendation: Skeletal muscle relaxants, steroids, enzymes, anti-inflammatory agents.

Specific Exercises: Chapter XV.

Thigh (Quadriceps) Strains

These are usually found in a heavy-muscled boy. Recognition, cause, treatment, and doctor's recommendations are very similar to those of hamstring strains.

Functional Tests: (1) Place athlete on table on his back, hold his ankle, slowly flex the knee and move the heel toward the buttocks. Watch the buttocks to see if they rise or tighten for compensating purpose. (2) Have the athlete try to do quadriceps (thigh) setting exercises; if he can't, strain is probably quite severe.

Specific Exercises: Chapter XV.

XI

Groin, Pelvis, Buttocks, Back

Groin Strain

Recognition: Usually occurs in the depression between the abdomen and thigh, specifically in the iliopsoas, gracilis or adductor longus muscles. Symptoms are tenderness, inability to run fast, jump, or twist.

Cause: Poor condition or warmed-up legs forced into a "split," poor posture.

Treatment: General Treatment Rules: (1) Alternate moist heat and microtherm with hot packs on groin and low back. (2) Often, because of improper body balance, one leg will be slightly longer than the other, usually the right. To check for this condition, place the athlete on his back with your thumbs on his ankle bones or measure from iliac crest to ankle bone (maleolus). To correct this, use what is known as the "x" method of stretching (definitely not an adjustment or a vertebra popping) (Figure 26). Have athlete on his right side, arm under head, knees drawn up (left knee flexed slightly more than right). With the athlete relaxed, rock his hip gently forward and gently push up and back on the shoulders.

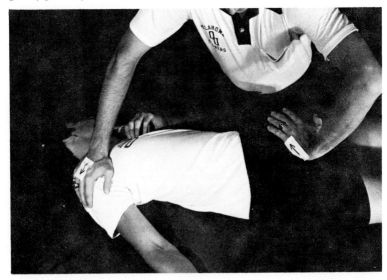

Figure 26

(3) Use patient's stretch (same effect as "x" stretch). Place patient on back on table; with his left leg perpendicular, lay it relaxed across body

(just hanging). Have him take a deep breath and, as he exhales, relax all over. Let him drop leg after each breath and keep shoulders on table throughout. (4) With patient on his back, slowly stretch injured leg out laterally as far as patient will permit then have him bring leg back to starting point as you offer resistance with body. (5) Standing beside training table, lift leg up and put foot on table (upward pressure tends to push twisted pelvis back in place). (6) Build up heel of shoe on affected side. Put a 1/2" felt or sponge heel lift in shoe on affected side. If both groins are strained, put a lift in both heels. This will shorten and relax the strain.

Functional Test: Rotate the foot laterally while holding the knee stiff. Lift the leg. If it is a groin strain, this will cause the patient pain.

Taping: Have patient standing, foot elevated two inches, buttocks dropped slightly with knee and thigh rotated slightly inward so as to pull leg toward midline of the body and thus shorten all tissues in the region of the groin. Using a charley horse wrap or two 4" elastic wraps or a slingshot (made out of line rubber — Figure 27), start the

Figure 27

bandage high around the thigh, then figure-eight it behind the back. The pull or lift is exerted when the bandage comes down across the abdomen and across the front of the thigh and under the buttocks. Many trainers feel it is better to start the bandage high around the thigh, then figure-eight it across the abdomen. The pull or lift is exerted when the bandage comes up under the buttocks across the front of the thigh and abdomen. Finish by pulling an elastic thigh cap up to groin. This will add support and also hold the bandage in place.

It may be necessary to use the above bandage over a pair of white cotton trunks to prevent chafing.

Doctor's Recommendation: Skeletal muscle relaxant, steroids.

Specific Exercises — Numbers 2, 3, 4, 5, 6 under treatment. Exercises numbers 4, 5, 6 under Hamstring Exercises and number 2, 3, 4 under Thigh Exercises. Also leg, groin, hip, back exercises in Chapter XV.

Lymph Glands

These glands are located along the lymphatic system throughout the body. Their duty is to clear the lymph of bacteria, preventing entrance into the blood stream. In athletics, they are seen as lumps in the groin, under the arm, and under the jaw. When they occur, check the area that drains into the inflamed gland. The problem may be due to a local or chronic infection. Consult the physician immediately.

Blow to Testicles

A common painful injury.

Treatment: Be sure there is no abdominal injury. (1) Lift the relaxed athlete (Figure 28) four to six inches and drop him and repeat.

Figure 28

Object is to eliminate the muscular spasm by the sudden "jar." (2) Keep athlete on his back and push knees up to chin keeping them 15 inches apart. (3) Loosen belt. (4) Apply cold towel to testicles. **NEVER** use heat.

Jock Itch

An irritation (dermatitis) in the region of the groin: redness, swelling, heat and pain.

Treatment: (1) Make sure there is no soap on the area; irrigate thoroughly with water. (2) Apply Tinactin or Micatin. (3) Do not allow player to wear jockey shorts. (4) In competition, be sure he wears a soft-pouched athletic supporter, over white trunks if you wish.

Crabs

A form of body lice that resembles a crab and clutches the skin very closely, found usually in pubic area, under the arm and possibly on the abodomen. Bite produces intense itching. Contracted from toilet seats, benches, clothes, sexual relationships.

Treatment: Kwell lotion or shampoo.

Hemorrhoid - Piles

Are dilated veins in the lower inch or two of the rectum. They are usually caused by constipation or strain, possibly along with a hereditary weakness. There are two types: (1) small inflamed hemorrhoid, close to outlet. Physician may use suppository or simple incision and remove clot. (2) Vein enlargment, higher in rectum. Usually requires surgery.

Treatment - Keep the bowels open and loose (prunes, fruit). Wash the area at least once a day and use soft toilet tissue. To temporarily relieve the itching, use a commercial hemorrhoid ointment. Send athlete to team physician.

Hip Pointer (Bruised Crest of Ilium)

Recognition - A very painful injury. A bruising or tearing of the muscle fibers and attachments along the crest of the ilium. The bone may also be bruised or chipped. It will be painful for the athlete to cough, sneeze, laugh, twist or bend his body away from the injury.

Cause - A severe blow.

Treatment - Immediate application of ice. Follow with general treatment rules. This injury is very slow in responding to treatment.

Taping Method - Athlete stands, leaning toward injury. Use 2'' tape and place vertical strips (not showing) approximately 6 inches

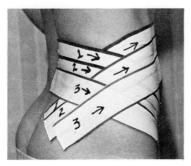

Figure 29 a

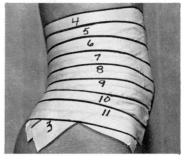

Figure 29 b

above and below the injury (Figure 29). Do not completely cover the buttocks as it will interfere with the motion of the thigh. Place diagonal strips over the vertical strips, then horizontal strips over the diagonal strips if you wish. Anchor the tape with an elastic figure-eight bandage as used in groin strain. (Refer to Figure 27)

Apply a pad to injured area before taping. It may be necessary to build up a hip pad with foam to take pressure off the injury.

Doctor's Recommendation - Steroids, enzymes, local anesthetic, skeletal muscle relaxants.

Protective Equipment - Crest of ilium pad.

Low Back Strain (Sacro-Iliac)

Pain in lumbo-sacral area, in sacro-iliac area or perhaps in region of 11-12 thoracic vertebrae. Pain may go down back of leg.

Cause - Lifting a heavy object improperly, sleeping on a soft bed, a twisting fall, lifting and bending, one leg shorter than the other.

Prevention - When lifting an object bend at the legs, not the back, and use the legs for lifting instead of the back.

Diagnostic Procedures - (1) Bend sidewards; back muscles on affected side will remain in spasm. (2) Limit trunk-bending. Bend from hips, keeping spine rigid. (3) To diagnose side of low back pain, with patient on back, grasp under both of his flexed knees and lift legs, swing raised hips from side to side; pain should develop. (4) To diagnose side of sacro-iliac sprain, have patient lie on back with legs extended. Keeping knee straight, flex one leg at hip. Flexion will be limited on side of strain.

Treatment - Ice massage; alternate whirlpool, microtherm, sound, and analgesic balm packs; back brace; sleeping on a board bed; a heel lift on short leg; traction and steam packs.

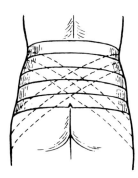

Figure 30. Taping for low back strain.

Taping Method (Figure 30) - Have athlete bend slightly forward with heels together and toes at a 45-degree angle. Using a basketweave technique (dotted lines) alternate several strips of 2'' tape from the buttocks angling up and across the back. Then, starting at the buttocks with horizontal strips overlap one another and extend up the back. For a sacro-iliac, place a felt pad under the above tape to give additional relief. Apply a 4'' elastic bandage over the tape.

Doctor's Recommendation - skeletal muscle relaxants, enzymes, local anesthetics.

Stretching Exercises - Chapter XV.

1. Follow number 3 and 4 under diagnostic procedure.
2. See Figure 26 and #4. (Patient's stretch under groin strains).
3. With athlete on back, grasp ankle and flex leg until knee almost touches stomach. Rotate knee in wide inward and outward circles.

4. Follow #3, only work with forearm under both knees, bring knees to chest and rotate.

5. Turn player on stomach, reach across the table and place hand on groin and lift up; at same time, place other hand below far shoulder blade with downward pressure.

6. Have player on back, knees bent and feet close to buttocks; bring right knee up to left shoulder and back to starting position. Repeat 12 times with each leg.

7. Keep patient on back, flex leg on involved side as far as possible and then suddenly extend.

8. Have player, on back or standing, pull in stomach and buttocks (gluteus) muscles and tighten them as if he were holding a dime between the buttocks, then throw hips forward (roll hips under).

Low Back Bruise

Treatment - Follow general treatment rules, alternating moist heat and microtherm with ultrasound. Use analgesic balm packs between treatments. Taping and doctor's recommendations same as for low back strain.

Protective Equipment - Back pad, back brace.

Fibrositis (Lumbago)

Fibrositis is an inflammation of connective tissue, muscle fibers, muscle sheaths, etc. often traced to bad teeth. There is usually in the area a soft swelling or knot which presses on nerves and causes pain. It can occur anywhere in the body where there are muscles. Most common site is between shoulder blades (called fibrositis) but when it occurs in the lumbar region, it is called lumbago. It is also a common cause of stiff neck.

Treatment - Heat, massage, ultrasound and steam bath.

Doctor's Recommendation - Skeletal muscle relaxants, enzymes, local anesthetics.

Transverse Process

Projects from either side of each vertebra, a muscle attachment. It may be bruised or broken or muscles may be pulled from their attachment.

Recognition - Pain and muscle spasm in the area (similar to low back strain) with a possible shooting pain down the back of the leg. It's definitely an injury that should be taken care of by the team physician.

Taping and Protective Equipment - Same as for low back strain.

Slipped Disc

Recognition - An elastic disc of cartilage located between vertebrae. Injury usually occurs between the third, fourth, or fifth lumbar vertebra. The symptoms are similar to acute sacro-iliac sprain; sciatic neuritis (aching, gnawing pain along course of nerve-back of leg); tingling, numbness of leg, foot, and toes; foot drop; pain outside of lower leg (knee to calf); weakness of foot; atrophy of thigh and especially calf. (Figure 31).

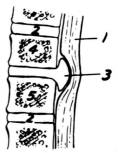

Figure 31. Normal and Abnormal Intervertebral Discs. (1) Spinal cord and nerve roots. (2) Normal intervertebral discs. (3) Disc has been rputured into spinal cord, causing pressure on the nerves, etc. (4-5) Fourth and Fifth lumbar vertebrae.

Treatment - Definitely a problem for the team physician, X-ray, traction, surgery, or perhaps microtherm, whirlpool, ultrasound, manipulation and rehabilitative exercises (Chapter XV).

Taping - Same as low back strain, perhaps a back corset.

Broken Back

If in doubt or if patient is unconscious, call the team physician immediately. Treat as a broken neck if not sure (Chapter XIII). If both back and neck are broken, treat as a broken neck. If sufficient help or material is not available to move the patient or if you are not sure, cover him with a blanket and wait for adequate help. It is better to do nothing than to do harm.

Recognition - If patient is conscious, ask questions; he may complain of severe pain along his spine (tenderness, deformity); he may complain of inability to move some part of his body; injury to spine may result in paralysis of body below the point of injury (if he can move his fingers, but not his feet or toes, suspect a broken back); have him follow your finger with his eyes.

Transportation - Move patient with the least rotation of his body possible for fear of creating or causing additional neurological damage. In other words, place him on the stretcher in a position as close as possible to the position in which he was found. If it is necessary to change the patient's position (vomiting, etc.) he should be transported lying on his stomach.

In placing a patient on a stretcher, have at least three persons to help and do not start until everyone knows what he is going to do. Place the stretcher as close to the patient as possible, with one person holding the patient's head, another his shoulders, and another his hips. At a pre-arranged signal gently lift the patient so the stretcher can be slid under him or, if sufficient help is not available, lift him onto the stretcher.

If the patient is on his back and it is necessary to place him on his stomach, raise the arm on the side next to the stretcher. Kneel along stretcher opposite patient (one supporting head), grasp his clothing on far side and roll him slowly onto the board, face down. Strap patient to the stretcher and remain with him until he is turned over to the doctor (stretcher bearers should not be in step).

If possible have a "scoop stretcher." In this way you can have an athlete on a stretcher without lifting him. The back board (or spine board) is also a recommended item to have on the sidelines. It gives a lot of support on the specific area you are concerned about. You simply slide the board under the victim, after you have placed a neck collar on the victim. Procedure is very much the same as above. Remember, great care is to be used in any instance. Do not hurry even if the official asks you to.

XII

Abdomen and Chest

Wind Knocked Out

Recognition - Often referred to as a blow to the solar plexus. Patient is on the ground, unable to breathe or talk and often making weird sounds in attempting to breathe.

Treatment - Place patient on back; attempt to determine whether there is any vertebra or rib injury; check his mouth for foreign objects and see whether he has swallowed his tongue (Chapter XIII). With patient flat on his back, grasp his ankles and gently press the knees into the abdomen. Extend slowly and repeat (no pressure on rib cage or vertebrae) or apply artificial respiration by placing thumbs just below the rib cage (no pressure on rib cage or vertebrae). In severe cases, use artificial respiration (Chapter XVIII). Do not at any time lift him by his belt or at the hips as this may add to the injury.

Stitch in Side

Recognition - Can occur in any athlete, but usually found among track and basketball players. Onset is usually quite rapid. Extreme pain usually in right side (stomach, ascending colon, and diaphragm).

Cause and Prevention - There are many theories: poor condition; constipation; accumulation of intestinal gases; salt deficiency; chronic problems; eating too much and too fast; greasy food. Stomach, liver, gall bladder are supported by small muscles and ligaments - if overloaded with food or bile they go into spasms; In some people internal organs (viscera) are loosely supported and swing when they run, which causes the stitch.

Treatment - Eliminate the cause. Slowly flex the right leg back to the abdomen, twist and stretch the stitch area, rest, relax, use mild laxative, and effervescent granules, wear a wind band supporter while competing, perform abdominal exercises (Chapter XV).

Spleen

Function - (1) Removal from the blood of aged or imperfect cells. (2) Defense against infection. (3) Storage of blood. The spleen is the largest mass of lymphatic tissue in the body.

Recognition - The spleen is located in the upper left corner of the abdomen, toward the back (side), just below the diaphragm and in the region of the ninth to eleventh ribs. Its main function insofar as athletics is concerned is the storage of blood. An injury is usually caused by a crushing blow, a fall or a faulty block. The immediate reaction is usually mild shock, tenderness and local pain. In severe injuries, there is usually a pain in the left shoulder which runs about one third of the way down the arm along with shallow thoracic breathing. These symptoms may appear immediately or anywhere from an hour to days after an injury. This is called a delayed hemorrhage. If there is any doubt in your mind, or if the athlete has any of the above symptoms, **rush** him to the hospital.

Kidney

Recognition - The kidneys, located on both sides of the spine, are partly covered by the last rib (from 11th thoracic vertebra to third lumbar). The left is slightly higher in the body than the right and both are approximately four inches long, two and one half inches wide and one inch thick. They can be injured by any type of blow and will cause pain, tenderness, muscle spasms in the area, shock, nausea, vomiting and possibly internal bleeding and blood in urine.

In the event of any kidney or back injury, the individual should empty his bladder into a bottle the first two or more times. If the urine is dark brown, if there is any trace of blood, or if any of the above symptoms appear, the athlete should be taken to the team physician immediately.

Shingles

Recognition - A very small, itching burning blister or "bleb" which usually starts on the nerve roots of the abdomen or side. The "blebs" fill first with clear fluid which later becomes cloudy.

Cause - The belief is that it is an infectious disease of virus origin (like measles or chicken pox). Contributing factors are: exhaustion, overwork, undernourishment, local infection, emotions, fever, blood stream infections, etc.

Treatment - Use a cleansing drying preparation and a light covering; ultra-violet light; microtherm; collodion.

Ribs - Broken, Torn Cartilage or Torn Muscles

Recognition - This injury is usually due to a blow or a twisting or stretching of the area (wrestling). These injuries are painful but seldom serious unless the lung is punctured (rare), or the injury is in the region of the spleen. The injury can be recognized by pain (on movement, coughing, sneezing, deep breath); tenderness; crepitation. A trainer can exert gentle pressure with one hand several inches in front of the injury and the other several inches behind the injury - gently pushing the ribs together. The patient may be able to feel some crepitation, (either cartilage or bone) or a sharp, stabbing sensation. If the athlete takes a deep breath while the trainer applies gentle hand pressure over the area of the injury, this should relieve the pain. If there is any doubt about the injury, send him to the team physician.

Treatment - General treatment rules with emphasis on microtherm, ultrasound and hot packs.

Taping - Ribs are a problem to tape as it is impossible to absolutely immobilize them. Also, because of the continual movement of the rib cage, the patient often suffers tape burns. Because of the above you may try a six-inch rib belt on most rib injuries. There are, however, times when it is necessary (wrestling competition, etc.) to tape the rib. When this occasion comes up, use the following method:

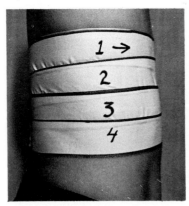 

Figure 32 a   Figure 32 b

(Figure 32). Have the athlete stand with arm raised and hand resting on top of head. Anchor two-inch tape at the spinal column well below the injury. Have the athlete exhale completely then pull the tape around (following contour of ribs) and across to the center of the front of the body. Repeat above (overlapping tape) until the entire injured area is covered. Cover the nipple with a gauze pad. If the boy is going into competition, it may be necessary to lightly encircle the rib cage with three-inch elastic adhesive tape to keep the two-inch strips from loosening and peeling. If the injury is a torn rib cartilage, place a piece of felt over the injury before taping. This will keep the cartilage in place.

Protective Equipment - Rib pads for protection; rib belt in place of tape.

Breast Bone Bruise or Separation

Recognition - The breast bone, technically known as the sternum, is divided into three parts: manubrium, gladiolus (or body), and xiphoid process. Any part of this bone can be bruised and, on rare occasions, the manubrium is separated from the gladiolus. The injury is recognized by pain, swelling, tenderness, deformity, or crepitation. Send to team physician if you have any doubt about the injury.

Treatment - Relieve the pain and tenderness with microtherm, ultrasound, etc. A six-inch rib belt with a felt pressure pad under the belt and over the injury may be used.

Taping - Similar to strapping for a sterno-clavicular sprain (Figure 33) only continue the basketweave down over the breast bone and add parallel strips to the basketweave starting at top of sternum and running toward the xiphoid process. Use felt pressure pad over the area of the injury if there is a bone separation.

Protective Equipment - Special home-made pad to relieve pressure while playing; rib belt; sternum pad; in some cases a clavicle splint will give relief.

Sternoclavicular Sprain

Recognition - This injury is commonly known as a separation of the collar bone from its attachments to the breast bone. This injury rarely occurs in mature athletes. It is more common in high school athletes. It is recognized by tenderness, swelling, deformity, and limited use of the shoulder.

Cause - Falling on the shoulder with a backward rotation, especially the tip of the shoulder; shoulder twisted backwards as in wrestling.

Treatment - Put arm in sling and send to team physician; general

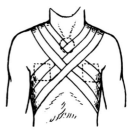

Figure 33. Taping for sterno-clavicular sprain.

treatment rules.

Taping - Place a felt pressure pad over the joint and tape it as illustrated in Figure 33. Cover the nipple before taping.

Doctor's Recommendations - Local anesthetic, steroid injections.

XIII

Neck, Face and Head

NECK, FACE AND HEAD

Neck - Strain or Sprain

Recognition - Usually in the trapezius muscle characterized by pain or stiffness. If pain is along cervical spine, treat as a broken neck.

Neck Tests:

1. Have the athlete move his neck through a range of motion. Look for limited movement as the athlete flexes and extends, rotates left and right, and bends the head laterally left and right.

2. Have athlete use same motions as above while you resist movements to check for weakness.

3. If the athlete bends his head to the right and there is pain in the left arm, or if he bends his head to the left and there is pain in the right arm, suspect a brachial plexus injury. If the pain is down the same side that the athlete bent his head, suspect a cervical injury.

Cause - A twisting or stretching of the neck muscles; sleeping with neck in a cramped position; a blow sharply snapping the head to the side.

Treatment - Ultrasound; microtherm; medocollator, massage, hot shower, hot packs in between other treatments. Traction and stretching exercises (not pops of vertebrae) as follows:

1. On Stomach - head on soft pillow, turned to right. Reverse hands (right hand on edge of right shoulder blade and left hand on head). Hold head stationary and apply pressure only on shoulder that is down and not out.

2. On Back - with head over edge of table and resting on your trainer's knees, place one hand on patient's chin and the other on his head. Hold head and neck in a straight line. Put head slowly through the following movements:

    a. Turn head to left and then to right as far as you can.

    b. Bend head to right and then to left.

    c. Force head to chest as far as you can.

    d. Force head back as far as you can.

3. In standing position. Have athlete alternate single shoulder shrugging, then shrug both shoulders together.

4. In sitting or lying position. Have patient offer resistance to the following movements:

    a. Hold head back as far as it will go while you slowly force it to chest against resistance.

    b. Turn head 1/4 turn right and then straight ahead against resistance. Repeat with head starting 1/2 turn to left.

112

c. Place chin on chest while you slowly force it to normal position.

d. Repeat b. only start with head flexed 1/2 right and left.

Taping - Most trainers do not tape this type of injury. However, some have had success with the following method. With player sitting on a stool with shoulders thrown back, use 1 1/2" adhesive, start with horizontal strips at hair line, and continue to bottom of shoulder blade (extend out to lateral edge of shoulder blade). Next, apply 2" diagonal overlapping strips starting above nipples and pulling diagonally across shoulder (near neck) and down back attaching below shoulder blade on opposite side. Repeat procedure, forming an "X" at spinal column.

Doctor's Recommendation - Skeletal muscle relaxants.

Protective Equipment - A homemade collar (made out of sponge rubber and felt), a rolled towel, or a commercial neck collar.

Nerve Injury to Neck

Recognition - Very often there is an injury to the neck and shoulder that leaves the characteristics of a nerve injury, numb with pins and needles or a burning sensation running down the arm to the fingers (similar to hitting the crazy bone). In all probability, the individual has injured the brachial plexus which arises from approximately the fourth to seventh cervical vertebrae and the first thoracic vertebra and is responsible for the nerve supply to the arm and hand.

Cause - A blow or twist that sharply snaps the head forward, backward, or sideward.

Treatment - Gently pull (traction), shake and rotate the arm; massage the arm, neck, and shoulders; apply traction to the neck, and follow all of the treatment discussed under neck strain.

Taping - Fold a towel and tape it snugly around the neck. This will keep the head from being sharply snapped in any direction and thus eliminate the pressure on the brachial plexus. Instead of using a towel, you can use a collar made out of felt covered with sponge rubber and encased in stockinette. The stockinette can be tied, thus eliminating the tape or a shoe string can be placed through the center of the felt and laced into the shoulder pads to hold the collar in place. Another method to eliminate lateral flexion is to cut a 1/2" felt pad and fit it from tip of shoulder to the angle of the jaw. Secure this pad against the neck and shoulder with diagonal basketweave taping.

Doctor's Recommendation - Specific exercises: Same as for neck strain.

Broken Neck

Read article on Broken Back, Chapter XI.

Recognition - Patient should be treated as having a broken neck if he cannot open and close his fingers rapidly; if he cannot grasp your hand firmly; if he cannot follow the movement of your finger with his eyes; if he does not show reflexes when hand is pricked with a pin (used if unconscious). If patient is unconscious, treat him as having a broken neck.

Transportation (Scoop stretcher or spine board, "back board") - Move the patient with the least rotation of his body possible for fear of creating or causing additional neurological damage. In other words, place him on the stretcher in a position as near as possible to the position in which he was found. If it is necessary to change the patient's position transport him lying on his back. However, if he is vomiting, he may have to be turned on his side or stomach. When moving apply gentle traction to his neck and keep his head and neck in the same plane as his shoulders.

In placing the patient on a stretcher you should have at least three persons to help, and you should not start until everyone knows what he is going to do. Place the stretcher as close to the patient as possible. Assign one person to do nothing but apply gentle traction to his neck and keep his head and neck in the same plane as his shoulders; assign one person to the shoulders and one person to the hips and legs. At a pre-arranged signal, gently lift the patient just enough so the stretcher can be slid under him, or if sufficient help is not available, lift him onto it. Move the entire body as a unit.

If the patient is on his stomach and must be changed, use a coordinated lifting roll as close as possible to the method described above when the patient was on his back, with one person definitely in charge of the neck and head.

When the patient is on the stretcher do not place anything under his head if he is on his back; if on side, keep head and neck on same plane as the shoulders. Place sand bag, rolled newspaper, bricks rolled in a sweater, etc. on each side of the head to keep it from moving. Fold his arms over his chest and secure him firmly to the stretcher with anything you have that can be used to tie him down. Someone should guard his head and apply light traction during the entire trip to the hospital (stretcher bearers should not be in step).

Teeth

Injuries to the teeth have always been a serious problem. If a tooth is damaged, do not apply digital pressure to test its looseness. See the dentist as soon as possible. The drinking of cold water or inhaling of cool air causes extreme pain if the nerve is exposed. Relief can be obtained by using oil of cloves and rubbing the outside of the cheek with ice.

If you wish to place a temporary cap on a tooth, dry the tooth thoroughly and then mold some warm dental wax, paraffin, beeswax, or candle wax over and around stump of the tooth. Another method is to chew two or three aspirins in some chewing gum and use this to cap the injured tooth. (Keep away from gums and do not leave on over two hours).

Chapped Lips

Usually the result of moistening the lips with the tongue. Apply petroleum jelly, inhalant, zinc oxide, or a commercial lip balm to secure relief.

Cold Sores

Many people feel a cold sore is a virus infection. In so far as treatment is concerned, the best success is with the application of Tincture of Benzoin, which forms a protective covering and keeps out air and moisture. Other treatments are: Effervescing granules, Kenalog in Orabase, and A & D ointment.

Dry Mouth

Usually due to nervousness, breathing through the mouth or drinking of milk prior to practice.

Treatment - Spray Spirits of Peppermint into the mouth; place analgesic balm (about size of small pea) on roof of mouth; use ascorbic acid lozenges; rub glycerine on inside of mouth; eliminate milk except at evening meal.

Pyorrhea

Recognition - A chronic discharge of pus from the gums. In later stages, the gums become spongy and bleed easily. This is a problem for the dentist.

Treatment - All cases should be referred to the team dentist. Treatments may include eating fresh salads and fruits and using a toothbrush regularly. Use an antiseptic mouthwash (hydrogen peroxide if bad, in later stages one part peroxide to one part water or a salt solution). Vince tooth powder (sodium perborate) may be prescribed by the physician, usually three times per day for one week, then one day a week. Vitamin C tablets.

Trench Mouth

Recognition - Any of the symptoms of pyorrhea plus red inflamed gums. Highly contagious. Refer to team dentist.

Treatment - Same as for pyorrhea. In addition, observe strict cleanliness with all eating or drinking utensils.

Doctor's Recommendation - antibiotics.

Dislocated Jaw

Recognition - Inability to close mouth and a dull ache just in front of the ears. Usually either one or both sides of the jaw will dislocate (forward). Jaw may be fractured.

Cause - A blow to chin while mouth is open; yawning; attempting to take too big a bite at one time.

Treatment - Wrap both thumbs and place in mouth on last two lower molars, fingers hooked under jaw. Press back and down with thumbs while pulling forward and upward (tilting) with fingers. As the jaw starts to return to its normal position, slip the thumbs out of the way to keep from getting bitten. It may not be possible to reduce a dislocated jaw without an anesthetic to relax the muscles. After reduction, immobilize jaw in a four-tailed bandage and send patient to team physician.

Protective Equipment - Face guard; rubber mouthpiece.

Fractured Jaw

Fractures of the jaw or cheek bone are very difficult problems and require the services of an oral surgeon.

Recognition - Movement of the jaw is painful and limited and teeth may not line up evenly.

Treatment - Gently close the jaw so teeth touch normally. Apply a four-tailed bandage and send to an oral surgeon.

Food - Malts (with or without eggs); concentrated baby food; mashed potatoes and vegetables; vitamins and various types of food that can be prepared in a blender.

Locked Jaw - Teeth

Cause - Blow to the face, blow to the solar plexus, or a muscular spasm.

Treatment - Be sure patient's neck is all right; if he is breathing normally, put him on his stomach which will aid him to relax and thus open his jaws; massage the jaw from in front of ears to chin, oral screw.

If he is not breathing, hyper-extend the neck and administer cardio-pulmonary resuscitation as indicated. If he is unconscious (caution) suspect a neck injury and use the jaw thrust method respiration.

Swallowing of Tongue

Cause - Same as locked teeth.

Treatment - If teeth are not locked, reach in and pull tongue forward with the finger or grasp it with a pair of tongue forceps. The tongue once pulled forward may "flip" back again. If so, once it is forward, hold it down with a tongue depressor, side of a pair of scissors, stick, etc. Turn the individual on his side to keep the tongue out of his throat. Keep oral screw and tongue forceps at your side at all times.

If the teeth are locked, follow the treatment for locked jaw teeth. As a last resort force the teeth open with an oral screw and then treat for the swallowed tongue.

If you cannot get the teeth open or the tongue out, roll the patient onto his stomach and apply the Heimlich Maneuver (Chapter XVIII).

117

Nose Bleed

Treatment - Place patient in a semi-reclining position; apply firm finger pressure on upper lip; cold towels or ice to nose, forehead, and back of neck; pack nose with tampax or cotton saturated in adrenalin chloride or hydrogen peroxide. Do not permit athlete to blow his nose. If nose continues to bleed, send patient to team physician.

Doctor's Recommendation - Hormones and steroid cream.

Broken Nose

Recognition - Deformity; gently move area back and forth and feel for crepitation; usually cartilage is broken away from the bone.

Treatment - *To Set* - Place thumbs on each side of the nose and with firm, light downward pressure (to relax and separate the cartilage from the bone) gently ease back into position. Place tampax in each nostril and a gauze roll along outside each nostril and tape to hold in place. Send to team physician and until completely healed; wear a "bird cage" face protector.

Face and Cheek Burns

Some individuals (especially those with high cheek bones, prominent noses, etc.) have a tendency to have the skin rubbed off their faces. To prevent this, have them rub petroleum jelly or a skin lubricant well into their skin before every practice and game.

Bruised Eye

Cause - A rupturing of the capillaries and small veins around the eye.

Treatment - Apply ice packs; do not blow nose as it may cause the eye to swell very rapidly. If so, suspect a fracture and send to a physician.

Doctor's Recommendation - Enzymes.

Foreign Body in Eye

A foreign body in the eye is quite common. Sometimes, it is possible to remove or relieve the situation. If not, or in doubt, or if it

118

feels as if it is still there, send the athlete to the team physician immediately; (patch over eye).

Dirt, Bugs, Etc. in Eye

If object is under the lower lid, it is usually easily seen and easily removed. Wipe it off with a piece of moistened sterile gauze or cotton applicator. If under the upper lid, draw the upper lid down over the lower lid and moisture produced by the eye may tend to make it stick on lower lid, or have patient look down; grasp eyelashes and gently roll the lid up with a match stick, etc. so the inside turns out. After removal of the object wash eye with Collyrium with Ephedrine, a boric acid solution, or a commercial eye drop.

Stye

Usually an infection at the root of an eyelash and should be treated by the team physician. To bring the stye to a head, apply warm to hot dressings. Relief may also be obtained by using any of the preparations discussed under eye scratch.

Scratch in Eye

Should be treated by the team physician. Relief may be obtained from any one of a number of ophthalmic ointments, a boric acid solution, or a commercial eye drop.

Lime in Eye

Not as prevalant as in past years as most schools are now using other preparations to make their fields. In the event of a lime burn, flush the eyes with a boric acid solution, a commercial eye wash, or two drops of castor oil and send the athlete immediately to the team physician.

Cut Around Eye

Treatment - To stop bleeding until patient can be taken to physician: Digital pressure over sterile gauze, hydrogen peroxide, gelfoam, or ice. To close the wound apply an adherent to the skin to make the tape stick and apply a butterfly bandage (Figure 2) or send to a physician for suturing. To seal the wound, apply a small amount of petroleum jelly across the incision and then apply flexible collodion.

Contact Lens

The lightweight, transparent plastic almost unbreakable contact lens has become very popular in recent years. The size has been reduced from that of a nickel to the size of a lead pencil. Some athletes prefer the larger type because they are not apt to jar out during a game, whereas others prefer the more popular smaller, contour corneal lens. Also, their wearing time has been increased from three to four hours to a full day or more.

Generally, the athlete can manage any problem that may arise. It may be wise for the trainer to carry a mirror in his kit to aid the athlete in adjusting his contact lens. Try the soft contact which is on the market now.

Wax in Ear

Never try to dig or pick anything out of an ear as it will probably only be pushed farther back and perhaps even puncture the ear drum. Ear canal is easily infected and can result in serious infections.

Recognition - Discomfort, deafness, roaring sound in the ear.

Treatment - Syringe ear with hydrogen peroxide. Drain out and follow with a half-and-half mixture of sodium bicarbonate and alcohol. Send to team physician.

Foreign Body in Ear

Read first paragraph under Wax in Ear.

Recognition - Discomfort (could be an insect, etc.)

Treatment - Put a few drops of mineral oil, baby oil or olive oil in the ear and let it remain for a few minutes while the head is turned to the side. Then, let the oil run out and perhaps the foreign body will come out with it. If a bug, use a light and it may crawl out. If not, send to team physician. Do not use water if the object is a seed or vegetable matter as water may cause it to swell.

Ear Fungus

Recognition - A burning, itching sensation. Very common with swimmers.

Treatment - Wash with boric acid and alcohol solution twice a day. Send to team physician.

Doctor's Recommendation - Alcohol.

Cauliflower Ear

Recognition - An ear deformed from an injury in which the fluid under the skin has solidified so as to suggest a cauliflower.

Cause - An irritation caused by a twisting and turning of the ears as in wrestling, from a headgear that has been twisted while on one's head, or from a blow to the ear (boxing). This causes a collection of fluid within the ear tissue which unless removed will form a cauliflower ear.

Prevention - Rub vaseline onto ears; wear a wrestling head gear.

Treatment - Application of a pressure bandage and ice. If fluid appears, have it aspirated (removal with a syringe and needle) by the team physician. Follow with:

1. Fit a piece of cotton or soft sponge rubber behind the ear. Place a soft piece of sponge or cotton over the ear and secure with an elastic bandage. Examine daily, but allow to remain on from three to five days.

2. Apply a cast to the ear by alternating flexible collodion and gauze, shaping each layer (four of each) to the ear. Keep the cast on ear for five to seven days until sweat and wax loosen it. Peel off carefully so as not to irritate the underlying tissues. Do not apply a cast while ear is still hemorrhaging.

Concussion

Concussion is merely a term applied to an unknown result of a blow to the head or lower jaw and this description is used until a more definite diagnosis can be made by the team physician. There is a momentary period of unconsciousness resulting from the blow (usually less than five minutes and seldom more than ten minutes). Even in the case of a so-called mild concussion, medical advice is essential as a safeguard against development of complications. Repeated small concussions lead to chronic more severe concussions. Watch the individual for twenty-four hours. You may even wish to awaken him

121

every two hours. A good rule to follow is that any boy who has a loss of consciousness for only a moment should be taken out of the game for examination.

Recognition - Following are some symptoms of concussions: loss of consciousness, a temporary amnesia, disorientation (will not be able to answer all present-day questions - temporary condition), headache (if over 12 hours, have re-checked by physician), dizziness.

More serious symptoms are - dilated, fixed pupils (moving finger test); pupils do not react to light; unequal pupils (be sure and report this to the neurosurgeon as they may go back to normal by the time the patient gets to the hospital); blurring or loss of one-half vision; loss of sensation in extremities; numbness; prolonged drowsiness; vomiting (especially if it persists or starts an hour after injury); convulsions; paralysis; clear fluid from nose or ear; bleeding from ear (an indication of skull fracture); coma.

Movement - Check neck, mouth and spine. If any doubt about the type of injury, treat as a broken neck (move lying flat on back, face up).

Treatment - Should be left in the hands of the physician. Apply temporary first aid; make sure air passage is clear; do not remove his headgear, have patient remove it himself; apply cold water and ice to neck and face; do not use ammonia inhalant while he is unconscious (may cause a jerk of head); administer oxygen; treat for shock (Chapter XVI); take patient to a hospital (ambulance) or keep him quiet in a semi-dark room.

Test to help determine if athlete should continue to participate:

1. Rhomberg's Sign - Feet together, arms down at sides, eyes closed. If athlete's body starts to sway or if he loses his balance, do not permit him to play.

2. Eyes Closed - Hands and arms out to side. Have the individual put index fingers together in front of him.

3. Eyes Closed - Arms in front. Have him try to touch tip of nose with index finger (watch his eyes).

4. Eyes open or closed - Feet toe to heel and arms straight forward. Check balance.

Preventive Measures:

1. Do not permit an athlete to enter a game until all major signs of a concussion have disappeared.

2. Have players wear rubber mouthpieces.

3. Provide the best helmets available.

XIV

Shoulder, Arm, Elbow and Hand

Acromio-Clavicular (Shoulder) Strain

Recognition - This injury is often called an A-C separation or a knocked down shoulder (if chronic). It can be recognized by pain especially if pressure is applied over the A-C joint; irregularity of shoulder tip can have an appearance of a lump on top (Figure 34) or a

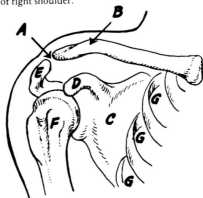

Figure 34. Front view of right shoulder.

A.   Acromio-clavicular sprain - note displacement (hump) on top of outer edge of shoulder.
B.   Clavicle (collar bone) where greatest number of fractures occur - at junction of two curvatures of the bone.
C.   Scapula (shoulder blade).
D.   Coracoid process of scapula.
E.   Acromion process of scapula.
F.   Humerus (ball of upper arm).
G.   Ribs.

dropping appearance. Other symptoms are the ability to move the tip of the collar bone up and down, pain if arm is permitted to hang at side, especially if light traction is applied, loss of motion as demonstrated by following functional tests: (1) Athlete is unable to lift his arm to shoulder level. He cannot comb his hair. (2) He is unable to touch beyond the small of his back. (3) He cannot bend elbow at his side and raise his arm laterally against light pressure exerted at the elbow.

Cause - Falling on tip of shoulder, elbow, or hand with elbow locked, blow on top of shoulder, improper-fitting shoulder pads, muscles of shoulder not developed, arm tackle.

Treatment - Use sling to support arm and elbow and refer to team physician. Observe treatment rules.

Taping - While shoulder is still in acute state, exert upper pressure on the elbow to aid in reducing separation. Keeping the shoulder in a semi-"shrugged" position (when shoulder is lowered, A-C joint will close) place a piece of felt 2 by 2 by 1/4 inch directly over the joint. Secure the felt firmly with a strip of two-inch tape, starting on the chest and pulling up and over the shoulder and terminating on the lower edge of the shoulder blade. Finish taping as illustrated in Figure 35 except do not use elastic tape around the chest.

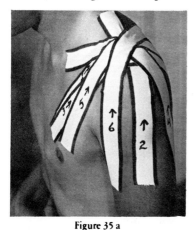

Figure 35

Figure 35 a

Figure 35 b

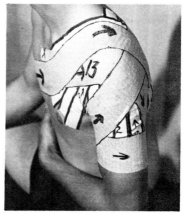

Figure 35 c

In place of the elastic tape, secure the upper arm to the chest and an extra large rib belt. Finish by placing the arm in a sling. Remove for therapy when physician will permit. When physician will permit activity, strap the shoulder as illustrated in Figure 35, anchoring around the chest with 3-inch elastic adhesive tape (gauze pad over nipples before taping).

Doctor's Recommendations - Skeletal muscle relaxants, steroids, surgery.

Protective Equipment - All-purpose injury pad (sponge) with hole cut to relieve pressure on joint (Figure 35b); build up regular shoulder pads to relieve pressure.

Specific Exercises - Chapter XV.

Bruised Shoulder

Recognition - Any one of many muscles in the shoulder area may be bruised. However, it is usually the trapezius or the deltoid. These injuries are painful but, as a general rule, are not serious and are characterized by the usual bruise pain and some functional disability.

Deltoid-Pectoral Injury - Bend athlete's elbow at the side. Have the athlete move his arm forward against light pressure at the elbow. Pain is a positive sign.

Posterior Scapular Muscle Injury - Bend elbow at athlete's side. Have player move arm backward against light pressure at the elbow.

Cause - Direct blow on top of muscle, improper-fitting shoulder pads.

Treatment - If necessary, support with a sling and follow general treatment rules.

Taping - Follow procedure in Figure 35 only place all-purpose sponge on shoulder with hole over bruise.

Doctor's Recommendation: protective equipment and specific exercises - Same as for acromio-clavicular strain except no surgery.

Shoulder Strain

The shoulder joint is held in place by a loose capsule supported by the tendons of subscapularis, supraspinatus, infraspinatus and teres minor muscles, often referred to as the rotator cuff.

Recognition - Swelling, localized tenderness over the joint, loss of force and function, an arm-tackle shoulder.

Cause - Tendons over-stretched (sometimes to the point of a tear) by a forcible twisting motion of the arm. (Received in an arm tackle, blocking, and quite often, in wrestling).

Treatment and Taping - Proceed as for chronic acromio-clavicular strain (Figure 35), with special emphasis to assist the capsule or rotator cuff tendons (anchor tape above elbow and *pull* to neck). Likewise, secure upper arm to chest with a rib belt.

Doctor's Recommendations, protective equipment and special exercises - Same as for bruised shoulder.

Bursitis

Recognition - There are approximately 140 major bursae in the body. Three of these lie under the deltoid muscle at the tip of the shoulder (subdeltoid, subacromial, subcoracoid). Practically any injury to the shoulder involves a bursa, some injuries more severe than others. In many instances, it can become a chronic injury. In some cases, X-ray will reveal calcification in the injured tendon or bursa. The pain is very severe (often requiring a strong analgesic) and is especially prevalent when one tries to raise his arm above his head.

Cause - Friction, bruise, irritation.

Treatment - Should be under control of the team physician. Rest, Ultrasound, Microtherm, analgesic balm pack, massage above and below bursa.

Doctor's Recommendation - Steroids, skeletal muscle relaxants, surgery, enzymes, and anti-inflammatory agents.

Shoulder Dislocation

Recognition - The shoulder is a ball-and-socket joint and a dislocation occurs when the humerus (ball) slips out of its junction in the Glenoid Fossa (socket in shoulder blade). Approximately 96% of shoulder dislocations are forward or anterior, when the ball goes under the Coracoid process. The athlete will generally hold his arm out with an anterior dislocation. Less common is the backward, or posterior, dislocation when the ball slips under the spine of the scapula. Posterior dislocations can often be recognized by the athlete holding his arm to his side with a bulge to the rear when looking from above.

The usual symptoms are: severe pain and tenderness over the area; a deformity of the shoulder - a hollow indentation where bone

127

should be, and a prominent lump (head of humerus under armpit) where it should not be; loss of function; elbow unable to touch side of body; hand unable to touch opposite shoulder; severe muscle spasm around joint.

Cause - A blow while arm is bearing weight, a rotation such as a catcher throwing a ball to second base, a twisting of the joint (wrestling).

Methods of Reduction - You should attempt a reduction *only* if you have been taught the methods acceptable to his team physician and also have his permission to attempt the reduction. Immediate reduction, if permissible, is advantageous in that it will reduce the muscle spasm and will not stretch the capsule and ligaments in the joint. If the individual will not relax and if the muscles contract, you should not try to reduce the dislocation but should send the athlete immediately to the team physician.

In a forward dislocation, the head of the humerus is in a position to rupture the brachial artery, vein, and nerves. Before reducing an anterior dislocation examine the nerves (brachial plexus) by flexing and extending the wrist and fingers. If numb do not reduce.

1. Kocher Method - Patient seated: (a) gently bring elbow in close to patient's side, forearm at right angle and straight ahead; (b) holding the elbow in this position, rotate the forearm outward almost to a right angle to the body. (c) With forearm held in his position, slowly and gently lift the elbow to an angle of about 60 degrees; (d) quickly bring forearm across in front of the body while holding the elbow in the raised position; (If an assistant is available have him place a towel under patient's armpit and lift slightly as you start section ''c'').

2. Prone Method - Patient on his back: (a) remove patient's shoe, place your longitudinal arch in patient's armpit, and grasp the injured's wrist with your hands; (b) exert a light, steady continuous pull on arm until muscles relax; (c) slowly carry arm toward patient's body with a slight inward rotation.

3. Mexican Method - Patient on back with arm out at right angles to body: (a) remove your shoe, place sole of your foot on patient's ribs just below armpit, and grasp wrist with both hands; (b) exert a slight pull on the wrist and at same time push the foot gently into ribs.

4. Athlete on stomach on training table, affected arm hanging down over side of table. Apply traction by: (a) Weights - 10 pounds for 15 minutes, or (b) Steady pull.

If an individual has a chronic shoulder (dislocated three or more times), he will probably be able to reduce it himself. This type shoulder will probably have to be operated on.

Treatment - In full charge of team physician. Follow general instruction treatment rules. Rest, microtherm, massage and rehabilitative exercises.

Taping - Follow Figure 35 using a 6-inch rib belt around upper arm and chest. Place arm in a sling.

Doctor's Recommendation - X-ray, surgery.

Protective Equipment - Shoulder harness to prevent raising of arm above 85 degrees; built-up shoulder pads.

Nerve Injuries to Shoulder (Chapter XIII)

Upper Arm Bruise - Myositis Ossificans

Recognition - A bruise (charley horse if on thigh. See Chapter X) to the brachialis anterior muscle (front side of upper arm), right where the cap of the shoulder pad ends when arm is raised. The bruise may rupture the bone-covering (periosteum) and liberate bone-forming cells (osteoblasts) which begin to grow in the muscle. This condition is known as myositis ossificans, which is a calcification in the muscle and may occur in any muscle in the body. It is quite painful.

Prevention - Shoulder pads that fit properly, or a commercially manufactured upper arm pad, an extra-thick layer of padding attached to the cap which will protect the upper arm when contact is made.

Treatment - Same as for charley horse in Chapter X. If myositis ossificans develops, treatment should be under care of physician who will take periodic X-rays of the arm to note the development of the calcium deposit. (Many people have good luck with ultrasound). It is usually two to three weeks before a shadow will appear on the X-ray film and, by five or six weeks, there will be evidence of bone formation. By the end of five or six months, the arm will be quite painful as a bursa has probably been formed between the new bone-deposit and the muscle (bursitis). It is not uncommon for the new bone-deposit to attach to the bone of the upper arm.

Doctor's Recommendation - Enzymes, surgery (has been quite successful).

Protective Equipment - See prevention; make a protective cup out of fiber glass and tape to arm; insert a fiber pad in a sponge rubber knee pad and have athlete wear it on upper arm at all times.

Strains and Hyperextension of Elbow

Recognition - See tests for hyperextended knee in Chapter X. Flex elbow to 90 degrees and flex and extend fingers; pain will be felt in muscle attachments.

Cause - Falling on extended arm, elbow bent backwards, a twisting of a joint.

Treatment - Follow treatment rules.

Taping - Bend elbow from 15 to 45 degrees and tape same as for an over-extended knee (Chapter X).

Doctor's Recommendation - Steroids, enzymes, and anti-inflammatory agents.

Protective Equipment - Hockey elbow pad, foam rubber (plastic) padding.

Specific Exercises - Chapter XV.

Fluid on Elbow

Same as treatment for fluid on knee (Chapter X). Same protective equipment as for hyperextended elbow.

Bone Chips on Elbow

Work bone chips out of joint and treat as any bruise. Protect with hockey elbow pad or foam rubber elbow pad. Surgery after the season is over.

Tendonitis - Refer to Chapter IX.

Tennis Elbow - Pitcher's Elbow

Recognition - Dull or sharp pain over lateral condyle of humerus; pain and weakness down forearm when lifting an object with forearm (palm down, pronation) and the elbow fully or partially extended. Pain is absent when lifting with palm up (supination). Individual may complain that condition feels like rheumatism in the arm and elbow. *Cause* - Authorities do not agree as it is often found in baseball, golf, handball, tennis, etc. players as well as in painters, carpenters, welders, etc. One theory is that it is caused by a twisting motion when player is inadequately warmed up and thus affects the pronater teres muscle. Another theory is that it is caused by a forced rotation of the forearm (palm up and palm down) with elbow extended. It is not associated with a bruise, but is usually prevalent after activity.

Treatment - Splint elbow and wrist. Remove splint for daily therapy. Sound and microtherm.

Doctor's Recommendation - Steroids, enzymes, surgery, and anti-inflammatory agents.

Dislocated Elbow

Recognition - Pain, deformity, inability to bend at joint. Usually a backward displacement of the ulna and radius (forearm) at elbow joint. Sometimes the radius only is dislocated and if so, this is forward.

Cause - A violent twist of the forearm; fall on the hand.

Reduction - Extremely difficult to set. Rarely possible without anesthesia. Never attempt to reduce without adequate medical aid except in a rare emergency. It is better to place the arm in a splint and take patient to a hospital and then help the physician with the reduction.

Emergency Reduction - Patient on back. Assistant holds patient's arm under armpit. Doctor will grasp wrist and gently pull the arm as he works the bone into place with the other hand.

Treatment - Pressure, ice, splint, and treatment by physician. If arm is put in a cast forearm muscles can be exercised by gripping a ball until cast is removed.

Doctor's Recommendation - Steroids, enzymes.

Special Exercises - Chapter XV.

Colles' Fracture

The most common type of forearm fracture is one at the lower end of the radius (in region of wrist, behind thumb) and is called a Colles' Fracture.

Recognition - Very often this injury is mistaken for a sprained wrist as it has the usual symptoms of a sprain. If there is pain, ten-

131

derness, or loss of motion in this area, the athlete's arm and wrist should be x-rayed.

Cause - Fall on extended hand in which the hand is forced backward and outward; severe blow (baseball), straight arm.

Treatment - Cast by physician.

Taping - Apply as for a sprained wrist and hand, with additional sponge rubber padding over and around the injury.

Protective Equipment - Fracture glove.

Specific Exercises - Chapter XV.

Wrist Injuries

The wrist is composed of eight carpal bones. It may be bruised, sprained, dislocated, or any one of the bones may be broken.

Recognition - In a bruise or sprain, the usual symptoms are tenderness, pain, deformity.

In a dislocated wrist, which is rather unusual, there is a strong resemblance to a Colles' Fracture. It should be placed in a splint, and the patient taken to the team physician. Treatment will resemble that for a Colles' Fracture.

In a broken wrist, the above symptoms hold true. Any one of the bones may be broken. However, it is usually the scaphoid (navicular) which is located in the hollow area between the base of the thumb (first metacarpal) trapezium (greater multangular) and the wrist in what is sometimes called the "snuff box." The scaphoid has a very poor blood supply and thus heals very slowly.

Fracture Tests - (1) Tap with finger or top of pencil on "snuff box" or over tender area. (2) Close fist and tap on end of knuckles. (3) Gently pull thumb and fingers.

Treatment - General treatment rules. If any doubt, send to team physician.

Taping - The first rule in taping the wrist or hand is to spread the fingers so as to increase the size of the wrist which will reduce the possibility of applying the tape too tightly. Secondly, always tape over gauze to prevent friction, etc. There are many ways of taping the wrist:

1. Encircle wrist with three to five overlapping strips of 1 1/2-inch adhesive tape.
2. Apply hand and wrist wrap (Figure 36). Using 1-inch tape, you can use this wrap to support a weak wrist and hand. To protect a bruised hand, place a piece of sponge rubber one-

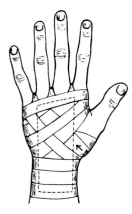

Figure 36. Hand and wrist wrap.

half the size of dotted line on the back of the hand and hold it in place with 1/2-inch tape placed between the fingers. For a sprained wrist (to prevent the wrist from bending forward), place a piece of 1/4-inch felt on back of hand (dotted line). Anchor between the fingers and cover with a hand and wrist wrap.

3. To prevent wrist from bending forward, place four strips of 1 1/2-inch tape from base of fingers to wrist. Fold ends of tape back to prevent slipping. Cover with hand and wrist wrap.

4. To prevent wrist from bending backward, place four strips of 1 1/2-inch tape from base of fingers across palm to wrist. Cover with hand and wrist wrap.

5. Use an ankle wrap in place of the one-inch tape in any of the above.

Protective Equipment - Fracture glove. Boxing glove.

Specific Exercises - Chapter XV.

Hand Injuries

The hand, as we usually refer to it, consists of five metacarpal bones. These bones may be fractured or dislocated. Dislocations, however, are rather rare. The symptoms, treatment, taping, fracture tests (add crepitation test), protective equipment and exercises are as have been discussed under Wrist Injuries.

Often when the back of the hand (or foot) is bruised, a *blood vessel* is ruptured. This is evident by a quick, large-sized soft swelling. Follow the general treatment rules of immediate pressure and ice. For overnight treatment, place a piece of soft sponge rubber over the ruptured blood vessel, bandage wrist and hand with an elastic bandage and instruct the athlete to keep his hand elevated. X-ray for fracture.

Thumb and Fingers

The thumb and fingers are made up of 14 phalanges bones. The surface of this area may suffer abrasions, bruises, or blood under the nail. These types of injuries have been discussed in previous chapters.

These bones may also be fractured or the joints dislocated or sprained.

Fracture Tests - Any of these bones may be fractured. Test the bone in the following manner to help determine whether the bone is fractured:

1. Gently pull thumb or finger, light lateral movement feeling at all times for crepitation. 2. Tap with finger over tender area. 3. Tap on end of straight finger or thumb.

Dislocation - Joint is usually dislocated backward.

Reduction of Dislocation - With patient's palm down, hold finger firmly just below dislocation with one hand; grasp finger just above dislocation with other hand. Place tip of thumb on "hump" of dislocation, index finger directly under dislocated joint. With index, second and third fingers grasping the injured finger, pull finger and at same time gently force the dislocated joint into position with the thumb.

Treatment - Follow treatment rules, then place in a splint (tongue depressors, metal, etc.) and have X-rayed. The following treatment is similar to the treatment of any sprain, with special emphasis on heat of any type to increase the usual poor circulation in this area. Also, the area should be exercised daily by grasping a rolled (4 by 5 by 1/2 inch) piece of sponge rubber.

Taping - There are many taping methods, a few of which are illustrated (Figures 37-40). Any of these methods may be combined with any of the other methods.

Doctor's Recommendations - X-ray, splint.

Protective Equipment - Fracture glove; hand bruise pads; any one

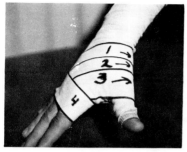

Figure 37 a

Figure 37 b

Figure 38. Taping for a sprained thumb. To prevent thumb from bending into palm apply 1/2'' strips of tape from base of thumb-nail down back of thumb to wrist. Apply a figure eight basketweave (Figure 53) over the above. To prevent thumb from going backwards, apply 1/2'' strips down inside of thumb to palm of hand and anchor with a figure eight basketweave. In place of tape strips, one can substitute a piece of 3/8'' felt in either of the above (Figure 49).

Figure 39. Figure 8 basketweave for a sprained or dislocated thumb.

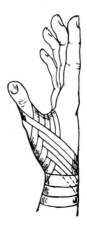

135

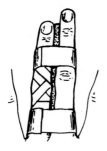

Figure 40. Taping for a sprained or dislocated finger. Flex the injured joint slightly. Using 1/2'' adhesive tape apply a basketweave over the injured joint. Place a 1/8'' thickness of soft sponge, felt or cotton between the fingers (optional) to prevent friction. With 1/2'' tape, tape to an adjoining finger which will act as a splint. Leave the index finger free if possible.

of a number of commercially manufactured finger splints.

Specific Exercises - Chapter XV.

Baseball Finger

Recognition - This is a tearing of the extensor tendon from its insertion in the base of the distal phalanx of any finger (distal joint), often referred to as a "dropped finger."

Cause - A blow on the tip of the finger which causes a forced flexion of the joint while the tendon is contracted.

Treatment - Place a roll of gauze bandage in the palm of the hand. This will keep the proximal interphalangeal joint in slight flexion and the distal (injured) joint in complete extension. Tape in place.

Doctor's Recommendation - X-ray, splint.

Protective Equipment - Commercial finger splint; a tablespoon with handle folded over the tip of the injured finger to protect the finger and the joint.

Specific Exercises - Same as for thumb and fingers.

Cracked Skin

Recognition - A peeling, cracking, hardening, drying of the skin.

Cause - Nerves, weather.

Treatment - Relaxation, glycerin, mineral oil, toilet lanolin.

XV

Rehabilitative Exercises of Specific Area Injuries

There are three steps in the process of rehabilitation: (1) a good surgical repair; (2) a good rehabilitation program and (3) the athlete's desire to recover. The rapidity of the rehabilitation of an injury is greatly determined by one's desire. One must work hard to reach his goal. With true dedication, one can rehabilitate almost any injury. There is a great difference between wishing and accomplishing the desired goal. Between the two lies a lot of hard work, both physical and mental. *Remember that what you can do tomorrow depends on what you do today.*

Criteria for Return to Competition

An athlete returned to competition before he is ready many times is hurt all year. Fulfillment of the below objectives prior to return will drastically cut down his chances of re-injury.
1. Full range of motion of the injured part.
2. Normal strength as compared to that of opposite side.
3. Normal endurance - injured part, cardiovascular.
4. Normal power as compared to that of opposite side.
5. Regaining of previous speed and agility: for lower extremity injuries - running full speed straight ahead without a limp, 90° cuts left and right from full speed without a limp, full speed carioca without a limp.
6. Normal size of muscular mass as compared to that of other side.
7. All exercise basically painfree (Exercise with pain increases recovery time).

In working with weights, you must remember that heavy resistance with low repetitions builds strength and high repetitions with light resistance builds endurance. Continue to add weights as lifting power increases.

When lifting weights breathe deeply on lifting and exhale on lowering. There are numerous weight-lifting formulas. Some of the more popular are:
1. Lift maximum weight 30 times in three series of 10 lifts each with a two-second hold and a two-second rest between lifts. Rest two to three minutes between each series of ten.
2. Determine maximum weight and hold it as long as possible (knees). Do three to five times.
3. Establish a maximum weight formula. Determine the

maximum weight you can lift (say it is 28 lbs.). Lift 1/2 maximum weight (14 lbs.) ten times. Rest and lift 3/4 of maximum weight (21 lbs.) ten times. Rest and lift full weight (28 lbs.) ten times.

4. Establish a heavy-to-light formula. Determine maximum weight and lift ten times. Rest and then lift five lbs. less than maximum ten times. Example: 30-25-20.

Be sure there is an adequate warm-up before each exercise period - running, stretching, rope-skipping, etc. - as well as a few preparatory repetitions of each exercise. Concentration and intensity are very important for a good rehabilitation program.

Arch, Ankle and Lower Leg Exercises

(Wear correctly-fitted shoes. Do not wear loafers, flats, or thongs).

1. On back or sitting. Extend foot as far as possible, pointing toes downward. Then flex foot as far as possible, point toes upward.

2. On back or sitting. Turn soles of feet inward so they face each other, then outward.

3. On back or sitting. Circumscribe small circle with foot, ball of foot down first, then in, then up.

4. On back or stomach. Start with soles of feet together, then breast stroke kick.

5. Sitting. Lay injured limb across opposite knee. Using hand forcibly flex, extend, invert, evert, and rotate the foot and ankle.

6. Sitting. Cross feet, press feet together, hold for five seconds, relax and repeat.

7. Sitting. Place foot on top of injured foot, attempt to raise the injured foot while resisting with the other, reverse and press down with the injured foot, hold for five seconds, relax, and repeat.

8. Stand erect. Walk on outside of feet, toes curled in. Or walk on supination board (triangle board).

9. Stand with feet one foot apart and toeing in. Rise on toes as high as possible (without pain).

10. Stand erect; then rise as high as possible on toes.

11. Squat to one/half knee bend without raising heels from the floor.

12. Ankle disc - round disc 14-inch diameter with 1/2 croquet ball screwed on the bottom. Place one foot near each edge of disc and make disc run around its edge on the floor.

13. Rock up on toes and back again. Hold weights in hands to increase resistance.
14. Stand on outer edge of feet and roll them back to normal again.
15. Stand on outer edge of feet and then go up on toes.
16. Alphabet - Sit on table, knee straight, ankle over end of table - print in capital letters the entire alphabet with your feet.
17. Run barefoot in sand, forward, backward, zig-zag.
18. Run backwards.
19. Jump rope.
20. Walk naturally. Just before foot touches floor point foot inward (pigeon toe).
21. Calf-gripper. Bring foot up to knee and grip opposite calf with toes and arch.
22. Stand, sit, etc. Heels together and toes out, to toes together and heels out.
23. Inchworm. Feet together and parallel, knees straight with heels and hands on floor. Take series of short steps with hands. Keep heels on floor as long as possible, until the body is prone, then walk back to upright position.
24. Ride a bicycle everywhere you go (stay out of cars).
25. Stand erect, feet flat on floor. Force knees as far forward as possible, keeping heels on floor.
26. Stand 30 inches from wall; move body to wall keeping heels in contact with floor at all times.
27. Sit on chair. Tap heel then to floor, etc.
28. Place golf ball under foot and roll it from toe to heel, etc.
29. Pick up marble, pencil, etc. with toes. (a) Place in hand opposite knee of good leg. (b) Place in hand behind buttocks of injured leg.
30. Sitting position. Feet on towel. Pull up under foot with toes. Then pull towel by inversion and eversion of foot. Place a weight on end of towel to offer resistance.
31. Sitting position. Hold one leg straight and slowly bring opposite toe up shin as far as possible.
32. Roll sole of foot over soft drink bottle or baseball bat. Place toes on a book and rock heels to ground. Place heels on a book and rock toes to ground.
33. Using weights, invert, evert, flex, extend foot (also while in whirlpool).

34. Run or walk up steps on toes (stadium steps).
35. Use stationary bicycle.
36. Swim (with kickboard).

Knee Exercises

The knee is just as good as the quadriceps (thigh) muscle is strong. It forms the first line of defense against knee injuries, and when it is weakened, strain on the ligaments develop. When the thigh muscles are strengthened, the knee joint is better stabilized and the incidence of injuries to the knee are decreased. You must keep in mind to work on the strength of the hamstrings. They are just as important to total rehabilitation as the quadriceps. The strength of the hamstrings should be as close as possible to the strength of the quadriceps.

Knee injuries seldom occur unless the foot is firmly fixed to the ground. Injuries in the pile-up may be greatly reduced by keeping the knee flexed.

1. Exercises while confined to bed or cast:
   A. Flexor. Flex muscles of thigh and buttocks and draw knee cap toward pelvis. Hold until leg gets tired. Do anytime: in cast, class, movies, bull session, dinner, etc.
   B. Leg Raising. With knee joint locked (either in cast or out), lift leg up (to right angle) and lower slowly - two minutes every hour while in cast.
   C. Resistive leg raising. Same as above, only rest the ankle of uninjured leg on the ankle of the injured leg and offer slight resistance to the raising of the injured leg.
   D. Extension. Lying on abdomen, keep the leg straight and lift the leg off the table as high as possible.
   E. Abduction. Lying on side with injured leg up, keeping the leg straight, raise the leg as high as possible.
Continue all of the above exercises after cast has been removed.
2. Limited Flexion Exercises:
   A. Sit on table with leg extended over edge. Weight of leg will gradually drop it into full flexion.
   B. Sit on table. Grasp shin and slowly pull to buttocks.
   C. Lie on abdomen. Place bandage around foot and hold in both hands. Attempt to flex knee by pulling on bandage.

3. Limited Extension Exercises:
    A. Standing. Place heel of injured leg on a low chair and hands on knee (patella). Slowly force knee back (extension).
    B. Lying on abdomen. Place a pillow under the knee, flex and extend the knee.
4. Lateral Leg-Swing. Place extended arm (laterally) opposite injured leg against wall. Swing injured leg out laterally, then across in front of leg as far as possible.
5. Gravity Swing. Sit on table and swing leg back and forth.
6. Resistive Exercises (See first few paragraphs of this chapter).
    A. Isometrics - each contraction should be held five seconds.
        1. Sitting, with a belt around the leg of a table and foot of affected leg, attempt to extend the knee. Use at least three different angles.
        2. Standing, use same technique as in 1, but attempt to flex the knee.
    B. Short Arc quadriceps. Sitting on a table with a roll under the knee allowing only 15-20° of flexion, extend knee with weight on foot.
    C. Weights. Using the same roll as in B, move forward on the table so that the foot is off the table and the knee is flexed to 90°. From this position extend the knee fully with weight on the foot. Keep in mind that the last 15° of extension are very important. (Execute in at least three series of ten, hold each contraction three to four seconds).
    D. Standing with weight on foot, flex the knee to 90°. (Follow same execution as in C).
    E. Sit on table and raise leg against gravity.
    F. Pulley weights. Flex and extend leg from sitting or lying position.
    G. Knee Press. Stand with feet apart, knees slightly flexed and hands on outside of knees. Press Knees together with hands, knees offering resistance. Repeat outward.
    H. Wall Push. Stand erect one yard from wall and try to force foot through the wall, keeping leg straight.
    I. Bed Lift. Stand with your back to an unliftable object which is about two feet from the ground. Try lifting the

object with the heel of the affected leg.
J. Bar Press. On back with feet under bar (weights on end of bar). Push up as far as possible, and slowly let it back down.
K. Isokinetic Exercise. In working with isokinetic resistance, use more sets and repetitions at various speeds. This is beneficial in that strength, power, and endurance can be increased without trauma to the knee joint or muscles.

7. Stadium Steps. "jog" up steps, and walk down (can add weight by carrying a dummy).
8. Knee Bends. Grasp bars (stall) with hands and do a 1/4 or 1/2 knee bend. (Do not use full knee bend or duck waddle).
9. Running. Emphasize leg extension by snapping the lower leg forward with each stride.
10. Run backwards.
11. Walk up steps backwards.
12. Ride bicycles (Buy an old bicycle and stay out of cars).
    A. Ride, with force coming from injured leg.
    B. Use stationary bicycle.
    C. Lie on back. Palm of hands under buttocks, leg straight and toes pointed.
    D. Same as C only add weights to foot.
13. Walk on toes. Can add weight by carrying dummy.
14. Raise weight high on toes up and down.
15. Heel-touch. Straddle position with arms over head. Touch right hand with rear of left heel, etc.
16. Leg swing. Lie on back. Raise leg to perpendicular with knee straight then swing leg across body until toe touches floor on opposite side. Keep hip and shoulders on floor throughout.
17. Hurdle Spread. Sit in hurdle spread position, with injured leg extended. Touch extended toe with opposite hand.
18. Quadriceps Builder. Sit on bench 3/4 inch behind knees, toes under stall bars and trunk erect. Raise body by contracting quadriceps and straightening legs. Weight can be increased by backward lean of body or by holding weights against chest.
19. Sit-Ups. Hook toes under stall bars. Sit up and touch right toe with left hand, and left toe with right hand.
20. Rocker. Lie flat on back. Raise legs to a perpendicular

position, grasp toes and rock back and forth.

21. Circle Drill. Lie on back with legs straight. Raise the injured leg (45 and then 90 degrees) and rotate it in small circles in both directions. Repeat with both legs.

22. Flutter Kick. Lie on stomach with legs straight and knees semi-locked. Move the legs up and down in the same motion as the flutter kick in the pool.

23. Canvas Strap. Sit with a canvas strap (which is attached to wall or table) around calf of leg. From this position, stand up without using hands.

24. Rowing.

25. Swimming (crawl, not breast stroke).

Two good signs to inform you of your rehabilitative status are swelling and pain. Either pain or swelling usually indicates that you are doing too much and should decrease the amount of work you're doing. Always use ice after every rehabilitation session to decrease soreness and possible swelling. In conclusion, always remember a well-developed quadriceps muscle is the best possible indication of a strong healthy knee.

Thigh Exercises

1. Practice any of the knee or leg, hip, or low back exercises which stretch the thigh muscles.

2. Sit on a table and permit leg to swing like a pendulum.

3. Stand, then squat until thighs are parallel to floor and heels and hands are on the floor. Raise buttocks with hands remaining on floor.

4. In a sitting position, grasp knees and pull to chin and then rock back and forth.

5. Lying on back, have teammate slowly rotate leg and, at same time, exert tension (pull).

6. Lying on back, have trainer flex knees as much as possible and at same time rotate knee in outward and inward circles.

7. Do sit-ups, bring elbow or forehead to opposite knee.

8. Stand with toes on end of a step (holding rail for balance) and then lower the heels as far as possible.

9. Cross the legs and then bend over and touch the toes with the fingers. Alternate the crossed legs.

10. Use functional test Number One as explained in Chapter X.

11. Lying on stomach or standing, with weights on the foot, flex the knee to just short of 90°, hamstrings relax and lateral sway may develop when lying on stomach. Read weight procedure at start of chapter.

Stretching Exercises - Upper Leg, Groin, Hip, Low Back

All stretching exercises should be done slowly, no sudden jerks or speeding up.
1. Practice all groin and back exercises in Chapter XI.
2. Sitting semi-split (Hips, legs, back, groin, knees), spread legs as far as possible and grasp ankles, keep knees straight and touch forehead to floor. Hold five seconds, relax and repeat.
3. Standing with legs spread and hands on groin, bend all four ways and rotate.
4. On knees with hands on groin, bend slowly backward.
5. Assume split position with left leg forward and (knee on ground). Support with hands on floor below forward thigh. Gently lower, hold five seconds, then reverse legs.

Hamstring Exercises

After each exercise, touch toes 10-12 times from a standing position as hamstring muscles have a tendency to shorten during activity.
1. Use any part of leg, hip or low back exercises that stretch the hamstring muscles plus knee exercise number 1A, 1D, 3A, 3B, 4, 6A-2, 6D, 6H, 6I, 6K, 15, 16, 17, 20.
2. Keep feet apart, bend over, hold five seconds, relax and repeat.
3. Stand semi-split (hips, legs, back, groin, knees). Standing, repeat above only from standing position (pull downward, trying to touch head to floor), hold five seconds, relax, and repeat.
4. Chest to Wall (front thigh). Stand facing wall with chest touching and feet close. Raise leg back and up. Grasp instep with hand and pull leg up as far as possible (head, back, and knee must not be out to side), hold for five seconds, relax, and repeat.
5. Knee Press (Buttocks, hip, and back). Lie flat on back, while teammate holds one leg down and presses opposite knee toward armpit. Stretch as far as possible, hold five seconds, relax, and repeat.

6. Table Sit (Hips, groin, buttocks, knees). Spread legs as far as possible. Hold back of table. Lower buttocks straight down slowly and try to sit on floor. Hold five seconds, relax, and repeat.

7. Knees In (Hip, knees). Sit with feet spread as far as possible and knees straight. Bend legs inward until knees touch. Try to touch the floor with inside of knees. Hold five seconds, relax, and repeat.

8. Inchworm (Hamstrings). Place palms on floor, two feet in front of feet. Slowly straighten legs until knees are straight. Move hands in closer to feet, keeping hands and feet flat on floor at all times, relax and repeat.

9. Hurdle Touch (Groin, inside thigh). Place inside of knee on table or chair. Touch floor beside foot with both hands. Hold five seconds, relax, and repeat.

10. Foot Shuffle (lower leg, knee, hamstrings). Stand back from wall with feet flat on floor. Lean forward, place hands on wall. Shuffle feet back as far as possible, heels on floor. Hold five seconds, relax, and repeat.

11. Hurdle Spread (Back, hips, legs). Sit on floor, one leg at right angles to body, inside of knee and thigh on floor. Keep other leg straight, toes up, back of knee of floor. Move body, chin to knee, hands to toes. Hold five seconds, relax, and repeat.

12. Touch Toes (back of legs). Stand erect with legs crossed. Bend forward without bending knees and touch toes. Hold five seconds, relax, and repeat.

13. Toe Balance (Back of legs). Place toes on end of step, hold railing for balance. Drop heel as far as possible. Hold five seconds, relax, and repeat.

14. Leg Shake (Legs, hips, back). Relax on table on back while teammate grasps one ankle and shakes with slight pull. Repeat with other ankle, then with both ankles.

15. Use the following exercises (Summer Conditioning Program-Chapter III): Running, Rope-Skipping, Side Bender, Knee Stretcher, Groin Stretcher, Bicycle Riding, Leg Flexing, Wood Chopper, Quarter Eagles, Trunk Twister, All Fours, Sit-Up and Paw Dirt, Mountain Climber, Leg-Back Stretch, Toe and Heel Dance, Sacro-iliac Stretch, and Leg Stretch.

Hip, Back, Abdomen Exercises

1. Practice all back and hip exercises in Chapter XI.

2. Practice exercises number 2, 3, 5, 6, 7, 11, 14 under stretching exercises for leg, groin, hip and back.
3. Hiplifter. Lie on back, feet drawn up to buttocks. Lift hips.
4. Abdominal strengthener. Lie on back, with arms across chest. Lift back four inches off floor and hold.
5. Eight Count Leg Lift. Lie on back. On count of one, lift legs two inches off ground and hold; raise two more inches on count of two. At count of four, legs should be at 45°. Open and close the legs eight times. At count of five, raise up two more inches; at count of eight have legs perpendicular, then open and close eight times. By the count go down to 45° and open and close and then on to the floor by the count.
6. Hip Rotator. With inside foot on a book and arm on back of a chair, rotate outside leg in forward and backward circles.
7. Bicycling. Lie on back.
8. Pelvic Roller. Standing and do the hula.
9. Sweat-Your-Shadow. Stand with your back against a wall, force shoulders, back and hips into wall.
10. Abductor. Lying on mat on right side, lift left leg from hip as high as possible. Repeat right leg.
11. Spine Bender. Standing on hands and knees, work spine up and down from hips to neck.
12. Concentric Roller. Support weight on hands and toes, roll hips in outward and inward circles.
13. Trunk Twister. Standing with hands behind head, twist trunk to right, left, and bend forward and backward and sideward.
14. Sit-Ups. Walk on all fours; practice rowing machine; stand and touch toes.

Neck Exercises

When using weights, use the 10-10-10 series. Increase weight as tolerated. Raise and lower weight slowly.
1. Neck Flexer. Lie on table on back with body off the table at the shoulder line. Start with head as low as possible and flex neck. Keep shoulders on table throughout exercise. Use weights.
2. Neck Extension. Assume same position as with flexer only on table face down. Keep shoulders on table throughout exercise.
3. Neck Lateral Flexer. Lie on side, on table with body off the table at shoulder line. Start with head as low as possible and raise head

147

keeping shoulders on the table throughout exercise. Repeat on other side. Use weights.

4. Dorsal Extension. Lie face down with body off the table at nipple line. Start with spine flexed (down) and chin protuding. Extend (left) dorsal spine and flex chin toward chest. Do not raise body off the table. Use weights.

5. Rotator. Lie on the table on stomach with the body off the table at the shoulder line. Hold head in line with the body and rotate to right and left. Use weights.

ALL OF ABOVE EXERCISES CAN ALSO BE DONE WITHOUT USING THE WEIGHTS.

6. Towel Resistance. Force head against a towel that has been placed on front, back, and sides of the head. Offer resistance.

7. Hand Resistance. Practice as towel resistance, only use hands.

8. Rotate and Stretch. Using own hands, rotate and stretch neck.

9. Head Glide. Stick chin as far out as possible. Return and repeat.

10. Side-to-Side. Place a book on the floor with forehead on book and weight supported on hands and toes. Rotate head from side-to-side and forward and backward.

11. Neck Stretcher. Use with and without rotation, as used in training room.

Shoulder Exercises (May also aid neck)

1. Chair Press. Bend knees so arms are parallel to back of chair. Grasp back of chair and press inward for six seconds.

2. Doorway Press. Stand in doorway, elbows straight. Press outward, six seconds.

3. Table Press. Stand erect. Grasp the corners of a table with arms straight and press inward for six seconds.

On above exercises, change position either up or down to exercise at different angles.

4. Ape Drill. Bend trunk forward. Allow shoulder to relax and slowly swing arm in a circular motion - clockwise, counter clockwise, forward, backward, and sideward. Later hold a weight in extended hand.

Weights. Use the 10-10-10 series. Increase weight as tolerated. Raise and lower weight slowly. (Use weights in exercises 6-12).

5. Forward Flexer. Raise arm forward, elbow stiff.
6. Arm Raised Sideward. Raise arm sideward, elbow stiff.
7. Arm Raised Backward. Raise arm backward, elbow stiff.
8. Shoulder Shrug. Shrug shoulder up, back, and down in a rotary motion. This exercise can also be done without weights - bed drill.
9. Supine Arm Raise. Lying on back on bench with arm to side, raise arm to perpendicular position. Use weights.
10. Horizontal Abduction. Lying on back on bench with shoulder at 90°, raise arm perpendicular to floor. Use weights.
11. Prone Arm Raise (Horizontal abduction). Lying on bench, raise and lower arm slowly holding at 90° angle to body. Use weights.
12. Prone Arm Raise (Extension). Lying on stomach on bench, raise and lower arm slowly keeping arm at side of body. Use weights.
13. Prone Arm Raise (Flexion). Lying on stomach on bench, raise and lower arm slowly with the arm overhead.
14. Prone Rotation. Lying on stomach on bench, flex elbow over edge of table, weight in hand. Move weight forward, backward, and upward.
15. Use wall weights.
16. Use overhead pulley.
17. Use shoulder wheel.
18. Wall Climb. Keep injured side to wall. With arm bent, walk arm up wall as high as shoulder will permit by alternately moving the forefinger and second finger. Lower arm in same manner. Lean toward wall as arm gets higher.
19. Towel Slide. Use same motion as for drying back. With one hand above shoulder, one behind opposite hip. Vary range and resistance by adjusting hands on towel; keep head and neck erect throughout.
20. Atlas Resister. Force fist into palm of the opposite hand. Offer great resistance with the palm of the hand.
21. Break Chain. In this resistive exercise, make-believe you are breaking a chain across your chest.
22. Leaning Table. With hands on edge of table and feet well back, rock from side to side placing weight first on one shoulder then the other.
23. Cross Hang. Hang relaxed from a crossbar. Do not use pull-ups.
24. Push-Ups. Practice: (1) Kneeling, (2) regular with back

straight, and (3) leaning against back of chair or wall.

25. Chair Balance. Support weight between the backs of two chairs.

26. All Fours. With weight on hands and feet, back parallel to floor, and head up, walk forward and backward.

27. With back to floor, abdomen flat, weight on hands and feet, walk forward and backward.

28. The Worm. Bend forward placing hands under shoulder (knees straight as possible), descend by walking forward on hands without bending knees until body is parallel and within a few inches of the floor, then walk backward to starting position.

29. Shoulder Roller. With arms to side at shoulder level, start with small circles (forward and backward, palm up and down) and increase diameter of circle. Also do exercise with arms to front of shoulder, and over head.

30. Shoulder Swing. Assume straddle position with arms over head, let right hand touch outside rear of left heel. Throw opposite arm upwards as high as possible. Repeat to other side.

31. Do rope-skipping.

32. Use punching bag.

33. Swim.

Elbow Exercises

1. Grasp wrist of injured arm. Flex and extend elbow (using force) up to point of pain.

2. Flex and extend elbow with arm in various positions. Thrust hand upward, sideward, forward, etc. full motion, but do not produce pain.

3. Sit on chair. Bend elbow at 90°, rest forearm on thigh, palm up. Rotate forearm to limit of pain, then place palm down on other thigh.

4. Stand two to three feet away from wall. Place hands against wall at shoulder level. Lean forward, permitting body weight to bend the elbows. Then press against wall and push to erect position. As elbow strengthens, move farther from wall. Also do with arm against wall to side of body.

5. On hands and knees, lean forward and bend elbows lowering chest to floor, then push back up.

6. Flex and extend arm in various positions, holding a light

weight in the hand. Increase weight as tolerance will permit.

7. Rotation. Sitting with forearm resting on table with the hand off, grasp a twelve inch bar with weight on one end. Rotate the forearm, palm up, palm down.

8. Grasp bar (five feet high) and with arms suspended, let the body slack backward so that the weight rests on the heels (well under the bar). Flex the elbows and pull chin to bar. Part of body weight continues to be supported on the feet. Keep body straight throughout exercise. Use both inward and outward grasp of the hands.

9. Indian Club Drill. Hold club in and between thumb and first finger. Combine small circles with large circles. The small circles will be above and the side of the shoulder and will alternate with large shoulder circle.

10. Have trainer hold injured elbow in one hand while full flexing your wrist (palm down) with other hand. From this position, extend the elbow, keeping wrist fully flexed.

11. With arm first at a 45° angle and then at a 90° angle, rotate the forearm to right and left with weights.

12. Pulley Weights. Increase the weight with the tolerance of the muscles and joints.

13. Carry books, etc. in hand of bad elbow.

14. Bag Punching. Use as patient nears complete recovery.

15. Grip piece of sponge rubber (4" by 5" by 1 1/2").

16. Door Knob Turner. Turn door knob. Bolt tightener.

17. Horizontal Bar. Support weight on bar and do push-ups.

18. Chair Bender. Lean on back of chair, and go down by bending elbow.

19. Pull-Ups. Practice with palm out and palm in.

20. All Fours. Walk in all directions.

21. Use Wall Wheel.

22. Rope-Skip.

23. Practice Rowing Machine.

24. Do Push-Ups.

25. Throw Darts.

Wrist, Hand, and Finger Exercises

1. Practice elbow exercises number 3, 4, 5, 13, 14, 19, 22, 23, 25.

2. Forced Motion. With opposite hand force wrist or fingers,

flexion and extension.

3. Broom Roller. With a broom handle placed on wall at shoulder height roll handle forward and backward.

4. Thumb Forcer. With thumb on injured hand, exert pressure on finger tips of same hand.

5. Spread Fingers. Spread fingers wide and then close into a tight fist. Use rubber band for resistance.

6. Sponge Grip. Using a piece of rolled sponge (4'' by 5'' by 1/2''), grip and release many times throughout the day.

7. Finger Push-Ups. Practice push-ups while supporting weight on finger tips. (This can be done on floor or against wall.)

8. Wall Walk. Place fingers against wall at shoulder level. Using fingers walk the arm up the wall. ;

9. Type.

The following may be done with or without weights.

10. Pronator Exercise. Assume prone position. Using a bar with weights on one end, start with arm off the end of a table with weight dropped as low as possible (supination-little finger side down) then pronate until weight is perpendicular to the floor.

11. Supinator Exercise. Assume prone position and reverse Pronator Exercise. Start with thumb side down as far as possible, then supinate until weight is perpendicular to the floor.

12. Ulnar Deviator. Stand with arms at side, thumb forward. Use same bar and weights as for Pronator Exercise. Grasp bar at end with weight dropped below little finger. Lift weight so it will be as close to side back of forearm as possible.

13. Radial Deviator. Use same starting position and bar as for Ulnar Deviator. Grasp bar at end with weight dropped below thumb. Lift weight so it will be as close to side front of forearm as possible.

14. Wrist Flexion. In prone position with hand far enough off table to prevent weights from striking table, grasp dumb-bell palms up. With wrist dropped slightly, flex the wrist upward to maximum flexion.

15. Wrist Extension. Use same position as Wrist Flexion except palms down. Extend wrist upward until searching maximum extension.

16. Wrist Circumductor. While standing, grasp a dumb-bell and rotate wrist in outward and inward circles.

XVI

Miscellaneous Problems Related to Athletics

Adhesions

Adhesions are fibrotic structures and are chiefly responsible for most of the permanent disability following operations, fractures, or dislocations. They are formed in and around the muscles, binding fibers and whole muscles alike. If adhesions should occur, there are four approaches to the problem: (1) surgical, (2) passive manipulation, (3) massage, (4) active or passive stretching exercises. You should consider surgery and forceful passive manipulation only after other measures have been exhausted. Active exercise acts in two ways to combat adhesions: (1) it increases local blood flow and reduces the tendency toward fibrous tissue formation; (2) it mechanically stretches and softens the scar tissue.

Air and Car Sickness

To prevent motion sickness sit in a well-ventilated area with the head held upright against the back of the seat. Close eyes. Sit in the front of the plane or front seat of the car. Prior to departure, take anti-motion sickness tablets.

Boils

Boils are infections caused by staphylococci bacteria. As an aid in bringing the boil to a head, use moist heat. Do not attempt to squeeze out the core. When the boil is ripe, spread the boil apart and remove the core with sterile tweezers. Use ethyl chloride spray to lessen the pain during the removal of the core. Boils which occur on nose, on upper lip or below eye are very serious and should be treated by physician immediately. More than one boil in the same area is referred to as a carbuncle. Treat all as infections. Apply an antibiotic ointment.

Burns

Bear in mind that the degree may not be evident for 18-24 hours.
First Degree Burns are superficial and characterized by a reddening of the skin (sunburn, mild scald, etc.). Treat by immersing in cold water as soon as possible. Prevent the damaged skin from drying out and cracking.

Second Degree Burns involve deep reddening and blistering - extend into deep layers of skin and do not require skin grafting (severe sunburn, blistering scald, etc.). May require medical care. Treatment: any of the first degree medications; sterile petrolatum; as much fluid by mouth as patient will take. If clothing sticks to burn, do not attempt to remove it. Simply cover with a dry sterile dressing and take patient to team physician. Opening of blisters is left to the discretion of the physician. Treat for shock and prevention of infection.

Third Degree Burns involve the entire skin thickness, with or without charring. These burns themselves, always never heal, require surgical care and usually skin grafting. Make no attempt at treatment, except to remove foreign material and cover with a clean or sterile dressing. Give as much fluid by mouth as patient will take. Remove to hospital in a reclining position with feet elevated. Treat for shock. (Wet dressing of a normal saline solution may be used in an emergency).

Colds

Colds can best be prevented if the athletes will abide by the following rules: (1) Wear a sweat shirt or jacket when not competing. (2) Take a shower after every practice or game, making sure the body (and especially the hair) is dry before going outdoors. (3) Wear a cap or hat during the winter months. (4) Establish regular bowel movements. (5) Breathe through the nose. (6) Drink plenty of water and fruit juices. (7) Get ten hours of sleep each night. (8) Wear clean equipment.

Constipation

Drink a warm glass of water every day upon arising. Attempt a bowel movement at a regular time each morning. Eat plenty of fruit (prunes every other day during double work-outs). If absolutely necessary, take a mild laxative. Massage the colon. May go to a high fiber diet (whole grain cereal, whole wheat bread), lots of liquids.

Diahrrea

Usually an over-the-counter product is sufficient; however, if diarrhea persists send athlete to team physician. Alter diet somewhat to high fiber meals.

Fainting - Dizziness

There are many different causes. However, most are due to a stagnation of blood in the legs (standing too long) or an accumulation of blood in the abdominal area (unpleasant disturbance). This causes a circulatory disturbance which in turn prevents enough oxygen from getting to the brain to maintain consciousness. The old method of treatment (head down between the knees) has given way to the more modern treatment of laying the patient flat on his back with the legs elevated. Apply cold applications to head and face. Open windows to get a cool fresh supply of air.

Frostbite

The long recognized method of treatment, rubbing after freezing or rubbing with snow, is no longer the accepted method. The American Red Cross now recommends that the victim should be made warm with extra clothing, and if the injured area is still numb and cold, it should be warmed as rapidly as possible by immersing it momentarily in lukewarm but not hot water. On the other hand, Dr. John T. Phelan of the University of Wisconsin Medical School stated that rapid thawing is the best first treatment because it shortens the time the affected part is exposed to cold and limits tissue injury. He states that rapid warming of the frozen part in a water bath at 109.5°F is the most satisfactory method of treatment. He further states that "increased tissue survival is not obtained when rapid warming is employed at temperatures a few degrees below 109.5°F."

Ganglion

A swelling of a tendon in which a clear, jelly-like substance (lump) accumulated in the tendon sheath. Usually found on back of wrist or just above instep, it is due to an irritation or strain. Treatment: tape a felt pad over the ganglion to help break up the snovial fluid-whirlpool and use analgesic balm packs. Team physician may aspirate and inject with steroids. Surgery is likely.

Hay Fever - Asthma

Patient should be under the care of team physician. When out in bright sun, he should wear dark sunglasses. To aid him in sleeping at night spray pillow or room with Sprahalant. To prevent secretions from nose, see topic on colds. If an individual has an attack, do not take him into a hot, steamy dressing room; keep him in a well-ventilated room; give oxygen if available; if at night, keep him away from cool, damp night air. Use drugs as prescribed by physician.

Headache

Many so-called two-a-day headaches are caused by a salt deficiency (see Chapter X - Cramps, Muscular). Other causes are constipation and improper-fitting headgear (see Chapter XIII - How to fit a headgear). Send to physician if headache persists.

Impetigo

Impetigo is caused by streptococci or staphylocci bacteria or a combination of both. It is highly contagious and is acquired by direct contact or a lack of skin cleanliness. Recognition is by red spots on the skin (can be anywhere on body, but usually on face, neck, ears, head or hands) which turn into small blisters, which fill with pus then break and form thick, yellowish-red crusts (crusts do not form in infants). Under the crusts are small red ulcers. Treatment: cover with antibiotic ointment.
Doctor's Recommendation - Oral antibiotics.

Insect Bites (bee, wasp, ant, spider, chigger, mosquito)

For any type of bite place an ice pack on the spot for up to one hour. This will give relief. Other over-all treatment would be to soak in a strong Epsom Salts solution, Caladryl, Ivy Dry, Nitrotan, Calamine Lotion. If pain persists refer to team physician. Also, in chigger bites, cover the area with nail polish or collodion. Treat chigger bites with Kwell.

Lime Burns

Wash with soap and water, then thoroughly irrigate with boric acid solution and apply an ointment as recommended by the team physician. For burns to the eyes, refer to Chapter XIII.

Mononucleosis (Glandular Fever)

Mononucleosis is a virus infection that affects the lymph glands, liver, spleen, and blood. The majority of patients are in the age group of 16 to 25. Its cause is unknown. Recognition symptoms are: temperature between 100° and 101°, chills, headache, sore throat, fatigue, swollen lymph glands, especially the cervical glands along side of neck, enlarged spleen, upper eyelids sagging, slow pulse and, in about five per cent of patients, kidney trouble (jaundice). The illness is usually over in about six weeks, but it may drag on into years. There is no specific treatment other than sending the patient to a physician immediately.

Pain - Methods of Alleviating

Ice, Aspirin, Ethyl Chloride.

Poison Ivy - Oak

A reddening of the skin with blister formations and intense itching. Wash with laundry soap and allow heavy lather to remain on area for 10-15 minutes before rinsing off. Thoroughly clean all clothing that has come into contact with the blisters or ivy. To treat, use five per cent solutions of Potassium Permanganate, wet dressing of mild salt solution, Milk of Magnesia, or Epsom Salts. Itching can be relieved by applying Ivy Dry, Calamine Lotion, or Calodryl.

Doctor's Recommendation - Steroid applications or injection.

Shock

Refer to Chapter XVI on Fainting.

Cause - Injury (self or sight of someone injured); bleeding, exposure to cold; exposure to heat or sun; poison; complication after operation. It may occur immediately or hours later and can be the cause of death.

Recognition - Face pale, in severe cases dull grey; finger nails and ears blue; eyes glassy, dull, no expression, pupils dilated; cold, clammy skin with fine perspiration on forehead and palm of hands; weak pulse; possible chills; temperature sub-normal; little interest in what is going on; restlessness; irregular and shallow breathing;

complaint of thirst; nausea and vomiting; unconsciousness; etc.

Treatment - Send for physician; place patient on back with feet and legs elevated (head low); keep patient warm; relieve pain or cause of shock; loosen tight clothing; use ammonia inhalants; avoid stimulants if shock accompanies hemorrhage, abdominal injury, fractured skull or symptoms of sunstroke. If possible, add sugar or salt (teaspoon to glass of water) to fluids. Orange juice, soft drinks, ginger ale, tea, coffee.

Sore Throat

Gargle with commercial products or gargle with 1/2 teaspoon salt and glass of warm water. If fever, see physician.

Staleness

A mental condition caused by overwork, monotony and boredom. It is usually a personal problem. However, it can affect an entire squad. The athlete who goes stale usually loses interest in his sport; cannot sleep; loses appetite and thus weight; is listless; is tight and irritable and may develop any number of illnesses. He often dreads reporting and dressing for practice. As a matter of fact, he may resent the entire program, but will not admit that he does.

It is the wise coach who will be on the alert for staleness. Following are a few methods of combatting this condition; do not practice too long; do not leave the game on the practice field (see Chapter IV - Practice Routines); change the practice routine from day-to-day. Add variety, perhaps occasionally substitute volleyball, touch football, or a good short swim for your sport; unannounced lay-offs; unannounced special treats (report no practice and give all a big dish of ice cream, etc.); holiday party for squad, etc.

Staleness is often the cause of the baseball player's going into a "slump" or the basketball player who all of a sudden just can't hit. Leaders in industry and business recognize this situation (yearly vacations, long week-ends), but many coaches do not.

Sun Burn - Refer to section on Burns. (Chapter XVI).

Sun Stroke - Refer to section on Heat Exhaustion and Heat Stroke (Chapter X).

Vomiting

Cause - Nervous indigestion; over-exertion; overloaded stomach, poor condition; partly digested food; virus; poison; spoiled food; drinking of milk too close to workout. Any or all of these conditions may cause a condition known as the dry heaves. Presence of blood indicates a hemorrhage. Patient should be taken to a physician.

Treatment - If an irritant is suspected, at first encourage vomiting by having patient drink several glasses of warm salt water or a glass of warm water with 1/2 teaspoon of sodium bicarbonate.

To stop vomiting have athlete suck a small lump of ice; slowly drink a glass of cold water with lemon in it (no sugar); drink a small glass of water with a teaspoon of spirits of ammonia in it; drink two or three drops of spirits of peppermint in a glass of water; take Pepto-Bismol; Kaopectate; or sip a cola drink.

Excessive Vomiting - Have patient sit or lie on right side. Give no fluids other than cracked ice. Apply cold towels to face and hot applications to abdomen. Call a physician.

Warts

Many types are thought to be infectious and caused by a virus. They are usually greyish, yellowish or brownish. Some juvenile warts can be removed with salicylic acid ointment or ultrasound. They may also be removed surgically, with the electric needle or liquid nitrogen by the team physician. See Plantar Warts in Chapter IX.

XVII

Administering a Massage

ADMINISTERING A MASSAGE

Massage is the scientific manipulation of the soft tissues of the body. A knowledge of anatomy and physiology is essential if one is going to properly massage an individual. Aimless rubbing may do more harm than good. Unfortunately, the art of massage is becoming a lost one in athletics, primarily because many trainers do not have the time and are thus leaning more and more on automation.

Physiological Effects of Massage

1. Increases the circulation of the blood and lymph.
2. Breaks up effused matter and hastens its removal (sprain, bruise, fracture).
3. Invigorates and stimulates the muscles and aids in the removal of the products of fatigue (lactic acid).
4. Aids in stimulation of large bowel (constipation).
5. Serves as a stimulant or sedative of the nerves and as an aid in promoting natural sleep and relief of nervous headache.
6. Often prevents adhesions. If adhesions are present, massage will aid in their removal.

Facilities

The "massager" should work in a clean, well-ventilated room (75 degrees F.) and carry out all massage under hygienic conditions. The lubricant can be almost any oil base preparation with an antiseptic content - mineral oil, olive oil, vaseline, etc. or any of the commercial preparations. In massaging the aged (to keep them in condition), many use talcum powder as a lubricant. The massage table should be of the right height for the operator (so operator can use his shoulders and back while massaging, without undue fatigue) and approximately 20 inches wide. It should be well padded, be covered with a sheet, and have a pillow available.

Aids in Massage

1. Try to relax the patient completely.
2. Use pre-warming (lamps) on the area to be massaged to soften tissues and assure deeper penetration with minimum force.
3. Have a reason to massage. Beware of the "goldbricks."

4. You should:
   a. Be as relaxed as the athlete to prevent fatigue.
   b. Have warm hands, remove rings from fingers.
   c. Strive to develop a soft yet firm touch.
   d. Have a smooth, slow, rhythmic motion.
   e. Swing from the hips as you massage.
   f. Let hands fit the varying contours of the body, with fingers pointed away.
   g. Always support the area to be massaged.
   h. Massage lightly over joints and exposed bones.
5. Do not massage over skin eruptions, infections, breaks in the skin.
6. Start all procedures moderately, build up in force and intensity and end moderately. Do not cause pain.
7. After each part of the body has been massaged (in a full body massage), cover that portion of the body with a towel.
8. Always finish massage by rubbing toward the heart. Return venous circulation.

Types of Massage

1. *Effleurage* - is mostly superficial and aids in draining the veins, lymphatics and improves circulation. Using the palmar surface of the hands, apply a firm, even-stroking movement toward the heart. The greater the pressure of the hands, the deeper the effect.

2. *Friction* - aids in breaking up deposits and scar tissue, loosens sore muscles, and stimulates muscles and nerves. Use circular, rubbing movement with tips of fingers, thumb or palms. Compress the soft tissues on the underlying bone. Use great pressure on adhesions, little pressure on soft tissue.

3. *Petrissage or Kneading* - aids in loosening up muscle and breaks up deposits of foreign matter. This method also increases the blood supply to the deep layers of the muscles. (a) Can be deep or superficial. Grasp mass of soft tissue, lift and squeeze simultaneously. Work hands in alternation. (b) Rolling. Grasp whole muscle and roll it on underlying bone, also squeeze and compress. (c) Wringing is exactly what word implies. Twist and wring the muscle in opposite directions. (d) Shaking. Place hand under muscle and shake vigorously (track and for relaxation). (e) Ironing. With palm, compress the soft tissue on underlying bones (chest and back).

163

4. *Tapotment* - is not recommended except in unusual conditions. Tapotment is a stimulating, invigorating, exciting type of massage rarely used in medical massage, a striking movement alternating hands with wrists and fingers relaxed, springy, elastic blow, not hammerlike. (a) Slapping. Use palmar surface of hands, like slapping one's face. (b) Clapping. This differs from slapping in that hands are cupped. (c) Hacking. Separate the fingers, hold loosely and relaxed. Strike with ulnar surface (little finger), giving a vibratory effect. (d) Beating. Close fits and strike with ulnar surface. Make blows elastic.

5. *Vibration* - aids in soothing nerves, increases circulation, and helps when used on internal, abdominal organs (digestion - constipation). Impart a vibratory effect to the fingers and hands by vigorously shaking the muscles of the arms.

Start all massages with effleurage and finish with effleurage.

In massaging for rehabilitation of an injury, perhaps 12 to 20 minutes is sufficient. In aiding a boy to loosen up before a contest (track), possibly a one-to-three-minute massage is sufficient, spending a little more time on stretching procedures. A tendency among many is to rub the race out of an individual's legs - in other words, leaving the event in training room.

A fast-growing practice in athletics is the "buddy system" of pregame massage. Players pair off and each lightly massages his buddy - after having received the proper instruction from the trainer.

XVIII

Cardiopulmonary Resuscitation (CPR)

CARDIOPULMONARY RESUSCITATION (CPR)

The goal of cardiopulmonary resuscitation is life support. Life support measures should be started as quickly as possible and continued without interruption until further care of the victim is turned over to trained medical personnel or until the victim is pronounced dead by a physician.

This support system can be divided into three simple steps:
1. Airway opened
2. Breathing restored
3. Circulation restored

No longer than ten seconds should be spent in preparing the victim. A helper can be assigned to do the following:

1. Call a doctor, first aid or fire department.
2. Check to make sure patient has not swallowed his tongue - pull it forward.
3. Remove foreign bodies (chewing gum, false teeth) from patient's mouth.
4. Loosen all tight clothing.
5. Remove wet clothing (if possible) and cover with blankets, newspapers, etc. to keep warm.

When you give CPR, the victim's head should be at the level of the heart or slightly lower than the heart. The victim must be on a firm surface.

Steps For An Unconscious Person

Tip the head back to open the airway, and check for breathing. Place one hand under the neck, near the base of the skull, and the other hand on the forehead. *Gently* tip the person's head back, until the chin points straight up. It is very important that the tongue not block the airway.

As you tip the head, put your ear down near the mouth and look at the chest. LOOK, LISTEN, and FEEL for breathing.

If the person is not breathing, give 4 quick breaths. Keep the head tilted and pinch the nose to keep the air from escaping. Cover the victim's mouth with your mouth. The 4 quick breaths supply the lungs with oxygen quickly. DO NOT allow lungs to deflate between those 4 breaths. Check carotid pulse. (To the side of the Adam's Apple).

Locate the tip of the sternum (Xiphoid Process) and measure up from the top about the width of two fingers. Put the heel of your hands on the sternum next to your two fingers. *DO NOT* put pressure on the Xiphoid (you may cause some internal damage).

Put your other hand on top. Lace or interlock the fingers in order to keep fingers off the chest. (You may hold them up). While standing on your knees with shoulders directly over victim's sternum, push straight down. Pivot at the hips and use your body weight to depress chest at least 1 1/2-2 inches. Keep arms straight. Do not jerk.

If the person is not breathing, but has a pulse, give mouth-to-mouth breathing. If the person is not breathing and does not have a pulse, perform CPR.

In one-rescuer CPR, one rescuer alternates between giving chest compressions and giving breaths. In two-rescuer CPR, one rescuer gives chest compressions and the other gives breaths. Since two-rescuer CPR is more efficient, it should be used if possible.

Combining Chest Compressions and Mouth-To-Mouth Breathing

In one-rescuer CPR, give 15 compressions at a rate of 80 per minute. Then give two quick breaths (full) without a pause. Keep repeating 15 compressions, 2 breaths, 15 compressions, 2 breaths. Measure up quickly from Xiphoid.

In two-rescuer CPR, one person compresses the chest at a steady rate of 60 per minute - slower than the 80 per minute in one-rescuer CPR. It is easier to time the breaths if the person giving compressions counts aloud, One, one-thousand; two, one-thousand; three, one-thousand; four, one-thousand; five, BREATHE.''

Get ready to blow before the count of 5. Start blowing early on the count of 5, because it takes a little time for your air to get into the victim's lungs. Keep blowing until the next compression starts. Then remove your mouth. If you get out of order, it doesn't matter if you give breaths after 5 or some other number, as long as you give *at least* one breath for every 5 compressions.

Changing Positions and Checking The Pulse

Trade places in two-rescuer CPR every few minutes or whenever a rescuer gets tired. The rescuer who has been giving compressions moves to the head and checks the pulse right after giving the 5th compression.

Heimlich Maneuver

The victim has something apparently lodged in his throat as he will grab his neck (throat) with his hands. The rescuer grasps him from behind, making a fist with one hand and clasping it with the other hand so that the fist lies thumbs side against the victim's upper abdomen. The fist is then pressed sharply into the abdomen just below the sternum with a quick upward thrust. This maneuver can be repeated several times if necessary.

XIX

Contagious Diseases

CONTAGIOUS DISEASES

Many common contagious diseases are known to us. Four are among the most common found among young athletes.

Mumps

Recognition - Swelling in front and below lower tip of ear, with headache, chills and possibly a light fever. Bright red pimple on inside of cheek opposite second and third molars. Saliva may be sticky and jaws stiff and painful on movement.

Method of Infection - Contact with case or articles freshly soiled by nose or throat discharges from case.

Isolation - Until swelling has disappeared.

Incubation Period - 12 to 21 days.

Immunization - Vaccine - good for life.

Remarks - After puberty, the individual contacting mumps should remain in bed because of possible inflammation of the genital organs. Defective hearing may also be an after-effect.

Measles

Recognition - Symptoms of a cold in the head with fever, running nose, sneezing, watery inflamed eyes. Rash appears on third or fourth day and consists of irregular groups of dull, red, slightly raised spots, usually appear first on the forehead and face, and spread rapidly over entire body. A positive sign is the Koplik spots which appear early. These are bluish white specks on a red background and are seen on the inside of the cheek opposite the molar teeth.

Method of Infection - Contact with case or articles freshly soiled by nose or throat discharges from case.

Isolation - Until rash is gone.

Incubation Period - 7 to 14 days.

Immunization - Good for life.

German Measles

Recognition - Rash (face, chest) usually first sign. Seldom cold symptoms as with red measles. However, eyes and throat may be slightly inflamed. There may be a slight fever. Glands in back of neck may be swollen. Illness is usually slight.

Method of Infection - Contact with case or articles freshly soiled

170

by nose or throat discharges from case.

Isolation - Until disappearance of the rash.

Incubation Period - 7 to 14 days.

Remarks - Disease during a woman's pregnancy may cause birth defects for baby.

Immunization - Gamma Globulin. Good for life.

Chicken Pox

Recognition - Perhaps slight temperature. However, a rash is often the first symptom noted. The rash appears as small pimples which soon become filled with a clear fluid and later become cloudy and tend to dry up rapidly and form scabs. Successive crops of these eruptions may appear up to the seventh or tenth day. The eruption is thickest on parts of the body covered by clothing.

Method of Infection - Contact with case or articles freshly soiled by nose, throat or skin discharges from case.

Isolation - Until crusts have dried.

Incubation Period - 7 to 14 days.

Immunization - None

Remarks - When the athlete has apparently recovered, examine his head for overlooked scabs and scales. Seldom any after effects. Highly contagious.

Glossary of Terms

GLOSSARY OF TERMS

Abduction - Movement away from median line.

Abcess - Localized collection of pus.

Adduction - Movement toward a median line.

Adhesion - Abnormal joining of parts together.

Adipose - Fat

Albuminuria - Presence of albumin in the urine.

Analgesia - Absence of sensitivity to pain.

Anesthesia - Absence of sensation (drugs, gas, etc.)

Antibiotic - A substance which interferes with the growth of bacteria or viruses, usually derived from other micro-organism (Example - Penicillin).

Arterial Bleeding - Bleeding from an artery - spurts.

Arthrodesis - Surgical fixation of a joint by fusion of the joint surfaces.

Arthrolysis - Operative loosening of adhesions in a joint.

Asepsis - Freedom from infection.

Aspirate - The withdrawl of fluid from the body.

Atrophy - Wasting away of a part-cell, tissue or organ.

Avulsion - A wrenching away of a part.

Axilla - Armpit.

Bilateral - Pertaining to both sides of the body.

Bursa - Small sac filled with fluid interposed between parts that move upon one another. Prevents wear by friction.

Butterflies - Upset stomach, caused by nervousness.

Cartilage - Gristle-like padding on bones at the joints.

Cellulitis - Inflammation of subcutaneous (cellular) tissue. Flat, red swelling.

Chronic - Of long duration, long continued.

Contra-indicated - Forbidden by peculiarity of the disease.

Contusion - A bruise.

Counter-irritant - Product which generates warmth in and beneath the skin by irritating nerve ends, thus causing an increased flow of blood into the area.

Cyst - A sac which contains a liquid or semi-solid.

Diagnosis - Recognition of an injury or disease from its symptoms.

Dorsiflexion - Upward movement of the foot.

Ecchymosis - Discoloration of the skin.

174

Edema - A collection of fluid in the tissue.

Etiology - Science of causes especially of disease - loosely used to mean "cause."

Extravasation - An effusion of fluid into the tissues.

Fascia - Fibrous tissue covering muscle and other tissue.

Fungicide - Agent that kills fungi and may also destroy bacteria.

Furunculosis - A systemic condition favoring boil (furuncle) formation.

Gastritis - Inflammation of the stomach.

Germicide - An agent that kills bacteria, may also destroy fungi.

Hematology - The science of the blood, blood-forming organs and their diseases.

Hematoma - A blood tumor.

Hemorrhage - Bleeding.

Hyperemia - Excessive amount of blood in any given part of the body.

Insertion - Point of attachment of a muscle.

Ligament - A band of flexible, tough, fibrous tissue connecting the ends of the bones. This is the stabilizing element of the joint or the joint capsule.

Malignant - Dangerous to life; invasive of a tumor; tending to invade adjacent tissues and spread to distant parts of the body.

Meniscus - Inter-articular fibro-cartilage.

Muscle Tone - Normal contractility and promptness with which muscles respond to stimuli.

Myoma - Muscle tumor.

Necrosis - Death of tissue.

Neurolysis - Relief of a nerve from adhesions.

Neuroma - Nerve tumor.

Occulsion - State of being closed.

Osteoplathy - Plastic surgery of the bones.

Pathogenic - Disease producing.

GLOSSARY OF TERMS

Peritoneum - Thin membrane covering the abdominal organs and lining the abdominal internal wall.

Periosteum - Thin membrane which covers bones and contains nerves and blood vessels.

Plantar Flexion - Downward movement of the foot.

Plexus - A network of interlacing nerves, similar to a cable full of telephone wires (Brachial, Femoral, Sciatic, etc.).

Prognosis - A forecast.

Resection - Removal of a considerable portion of an organ.

Sprain - A twisting of a joint, producing a stretching (strain) or tearing of ligaments.

Spasm - An involuntary, sudden contraction of one or more muscles (Example: leg cramps).

Sterile - Free from micro-organisms.

Strain - Excessive stretching of a part.

Superficial Injury - Injury to the surface, generally not below the skin.

Tendon - A band of dense, tough, fibrous tissue forming the termination of a muscle and attaching the latter to a bone.

Therapy - Science of a medical treatment.

Trauma - A direct blow.

Unhappy Triad - An injury to the medial ligament, medial cartilage and cruciate ligaments of the knee.

Unilateral - Pertaining to one side of the body.

Venous Bleeding - Bleeding from a vein (even flow).

Vesicle - Small blister or sac containing liquid.

Viscera - Large organs contained within the abdominal cavity.

PREFIXES

Adero - refers to glands.

Arthro - refers to joints.

Derma - refers to skin.

Dys - means disordered, bad.

End - refers to inside.

Hema - refers to blood.
Hydro - refers to water.
Myo - refers to muscle.
Neuro - refers to nerves.
Osteo - refers to bone.
Phlebo - refers to veins.
Pyo - refers to pus.
Post - means after.
Pre - means before.

SUFFIXES

algia - pain (Neuralgia)
itis - inflammation (Tendinitis)
logy - Science (Pathology)
ptosis - falling or sagging (Visceroptosis)
rrhea - discharge (Diarrhea)
osis - abnormal condition (Tuberculosis)
phobia - fear (Claustrophobia)
uria - excreted in urine (Albuminuria)
ectomy - removed (Appendectomy)
stomy - forming artificial opening (Colostomy)
tomy - cutting open of an organ or cavity (Tracheotomy)
lysis - loosening from adhesions (Neurolysis)

MEDICAL SIGNS AND SYMBOLS

aa - of each
ac - before meals
ante - before
aq - water
bid - two times daily
c - with
c;w - colored or white
dc - discontinue orders
dx - diagnosis
h - hour
hs - at bedtime
iv - intravenous

GLOSSARY OF TERMS

m.dic - as directed or prescribed
m et n - morning and night
no - number
npo - nothing by mouth
pc - after meals
pe - physical exam
qd - daily
qh - every hour
qid - four times daily
q2h - every two hours
q3h - every three hours
q4h - every four hours
rx - treatment or prescription
prn - as necessary
s - without
s or sig - dosage, directions
tid - three times daily

Index

INDEX

Notes

Notes